Diverse Leadership in The Foursquare Church—
What Would Aimee Say?

Diverse Leadership in The Foursquare Church—
What Would Aimee Say?

Angelia E. Waite, D.Min.

AWM Publishing | Madison, AL

DIVERSE LEADERSHIP IN THE FOURSQUARE CHURCH—WHAT
WOULD AIMEE SAY?

AWM Publishing
P.O. Box 238
Madison, AL 35758

ISBN 13: 978-0-9860988-2-6

Cataloguing-in-Publication Data

Diverse Leadership in The Foursquare Church—What Would Aimee Say? by Angelia
E. Waite.

xxiv + 198 p.; 23 cm. Includes bibliographical references.
ISBN 13: 978-0-9860988-2-6
I. Waite, Angelia E. II. Call, Dan. III. Diverse Leadership in The Foursquare Church—
What Would Aimee Say?

CALL NUMBER 2023

Manufactured in the U.S.A.   2023

Edited by Lois E. Olena

Dedication

My doctoral studies, research project, and this book are all dedicated to my family. My husband and three sons taught me to lead among strong men. I am thankful.

Dr. Jay, you are truly my greatest fan and life partner. I am thankful for your continual support, love, encouragement, and late-night confidante sessions when there were more questions than answerers. Thank you for being sensitive to the Spirit and always leading our family toward Him! I love you!

Benji and Mitra (my daughter-in-love), you two are some of the greatest encouragers I have ever known. You stood, believed, and allowed no room for doubt in my sphere while on this journey. I love and adore you both!

Chandler, our early morning daily talks of encouragement gave life to my soul. Our deep theological discussions on difficult subjects shove me toward God, and I am a better theologian because of it. I love you!

In honor of our third son, Ramsey (1996-2000), whose mark on this family will forever remain, this project is dedicated to you, my baby boy! I will always love you!

This research project and book is also dedicated to all women unsure whether they are hearing God clearly because His call and society are so often in opposition. May this project release you into complete obedience as you find truth in Scripture. He calls, He anoints, He knows you are a woman.

Contents

Foreword

It was a lovely fall day in North Dallas when I finished reading Angelia Waite's manuscript, *Diverse Leadership in the Foursquare Church: What Would Aimee Say?* for the first time. It was one of those days near the end of a semester when reading papers is standard fare. What I read in no way felt ordinary. As a professor, I know the difference between common and remarkable. I have certainly read enough academic writing over the years to quickly determine the quality of a student's work and depth of understanding. After only a page or two, I knew this project would prove interesting and thought provoking.

Knowing Angelia as a doctoral student over the past many years, I had grown accustomed to her superior work as a researcher and writer, but in addition to these qualities I had become acquainted with her heart for people and passion for ministry. She is a woman of deep conviction, believing that God called her. While working on a doctoral degree, she served the Lord by pastoring a church in a southern city full of male pastors. Having served as a lead pastor for many years, I understand the many challenges one faces in this role. I am keenly aware of busy schedules, unrelenting time demands, and ever-changing expectations from diverse constituency groups. Alongside the pressures pastors face within the local church, ministry contends with a culture fascinated with anything new that tantalizes with promises of personal fulfillment, happiness, and individuality of expression in its many forms. Angelia's work adds another ingredient to the mix—ministry leadership as a called and anointed woman. Ministry is changing, but many in church leadership refuse to change. This book addresses the incongruity of a shrinking number of female church leaders in a day when the glass ceiling is being shattered every day in the marketplace. Her work asks poignant questions we must hear and address.

It is fitting that this book is written by a woman who has served the local church as a pastor. She enters the arena of theological tension having a clear understanding of the biblical passages many lean on when relegating women to leadership sidelines. She is fully aware that well-intended people do not all agree on what the Bible says about women in ministry leadership. She tackles the difficult passages as many of her predecessors have over the past few decades. She engages the biblical texts and asks others to do the same. Leading theological voices, both male and female, comment on the important passages, and an increasing number land on the exegetical conclusion that women have always had a place of leadership in the Bible. She carefully examines those few Scriptures that seem at first glance to prohibit such leadership but contends that those passages should be evaluated in the totality of God's Word. Changing theological viewpoints is no easy task, nor should it be when dealing with such an important ecclesiological matter. Hard-fought change has occurred over the millennia, reminding us that adherence to biblical fidelity requires that we remain faithful to God and His Word.

Keenly aware of her own denomination's historical acceptance of women in ministry leadership, Dr. Waite asks why this number is not growing amid a culture of increasing acceptance of female leaders in countless other organizations. Today, only 9 percent of Foursquare churches have female senior pastors.[1] According to *Christianity Today*, "only 13.5 percent of congregations in the United States are led by

---

[1] "This is Foursquare: Cabinet Report 2022," Foursquare Leader, accessed August 3, 2022, https://foursquare-leader.s3.us-east-1.amazonaws.com/about_us/business/2022-Cabinet-Report.pdf, 4.

women."[2] Women comprise over 50 percent of our faith communities, yet approximately more than four out of five churches are led by men. Current statistics about women in ministry leadership reinforce the question why so few women are serving as lead pastors today. This book addresses many of the possible reasons why leadership disparity exists. As you read, ask the Holy Spirit to teach you (John 14:26), to grant you wisdom and revelation (1 Cor. 2:10-11), and guide you into all truth (John 16:13).

Jesus shares two parables in Matthew 9:16-17 to address the theme of a new pattern of religion that was incompatible with the old traditions represented by the fasting practices of the Pharisees and followers of John the Baptist:

> No one sews a patch of unshrunk cloth on an old garment, for the patch will pull away from the garment. Neither do men pour new wine into old wineskins. If they do, the skins will burst, the wine will run out and the wineskins will be ruined. No, they pour new wine into new wineskins, and both are preserved.

Jesus knew that unshrunk cloth would shrink when washed and would have a disastrous effect if sewn into an old, and therefore already shrunk, coat. Wineskins were made of leather, which was at first soft and pliable but became hardened over time and eventually brittle so it could not withstand the pressure of fermentation associated with new wine. These two parables reinforce the importance of knowing what is important and therefore essential to safeguard.

In the second of these two parables we recognize the vital importance of the wine and the utilitarian nature of the wineskin.

---

[2] Hannah McClellan, "Assemblies of God Ordains Record Number of Women," Christianity Today, August 5, 2022, https://www.christianitytoday.com/news/2022/august/assemblies-god-ordain-women-record.html.

Wineskins are important in that they house and transport the indispensable wine. A contemporary reader might conclude that the principle of these two parables was not exhausted with first-century application. The historical Church has been highlighted by the bursting of old wineskins and the need to find suitable containers for the new wine. The gospel is and will always be the indispensable element/message for the Church. Wineskins change. With over five billion souls in need of the gospel, every hand must be on deck, and we dare not relegate some to the sidelines without an honest evaluation of our theology.

> With over five billion souls in need of the gospel, every hand must be on deck, and we dare not relegate some to the sidelines without an honest evaluation of our theology.

Reading Dr. Waite's book will not convince everyone, but my prayer is that it will further the discussion and convince all of us to get this right. Too many women have expressed a calling to serve the Lord in positions of church leadership and have been stifled because of a lack of openness to embrace them as leaders. Read this book with a sensitive heart and remain open to hear the voice of the Holy Spirit as you read it.

A simple prayer goes like this: "Lord, I want everything that is from you, and I want nothing that is not of you. Open my heart to hear your voice." Amen.

—Dr. Dan Call
Director, Doctor of Ministry, The King's University

Preface

This book explores the problem of the underrepresentation of senior female leaders in the denomination known as The Foursquare Church. The Foursquare Church—founded by a woman, Aimee Semple McPherson—endorses women in every area of ministry through its positional statement and bylaws. An area of study will be to determine if the leadership endorses an egalitarian theology as this denomination has fewer female leaders than other denominations.

To address this problem, I first conducted biblical-theological research to identify female leaders in the Old and New Testaments serving in the same roles as men as the foundation for the project. Second, I conducted a literature review to investigate issues facing women in the context of secular and religious leadership roles.

Informed by these research reviews, I used a qualitative methodology incorporating two valid data-collecting instruments: a survey with fifteen closed-ended questions and sixty- to ninety-minute interview sessions. I then administered both instruments to five senior female leaders currently serving The Foursquare Church in the United States, exploring their perceptions and experiences in search of commonalities concerning the denomination's forfeiture of women in senior leadership roles within The Foursquare Church.[3]

---

[3] The term *forfeiture* in this study is not referring to *women* who have forfeited leadership roles but rather *the denomination's* loss of benefits of women in leadership at all levels to the same extent as men.

Acknowledgments

This study was an act of obedience from a seed planted thirty years ago in the heart of an unsaved woman by the One who carried and guided this project. I pray it brings glory to Him alone. I am also eternally grateful for my family and their endless support. Their grace, love, and patience sustained me through. I am thankful for a host of intercessors who prayed for me, warred, and encouraged me throughout this project without ceasing.

Thank you as well to my doctoral project advisor, Dr. Lois Olena, for her guidance, support, and critical eye into this study. It was a privilege to conduct this research project under your tutelage. Thank you for encouraging me to use my voice to contribute to the concerns in this project.

I am also thankful for my doctoral committee—Dr. Leanna Thompson, Dr. Dan Call, Dr. Robb Brewer—and the others at The King's University who assisted in this project.

Introduction

Jesus is walking along the Sea of Galilee, and He sees two brothers, Simon and Andrew, fishermen by trade, and says to them, "Follow me, and I will make you fishers of people" (Matt 4:19). Jesus promised to make them fishers of men upon one simple condition—that they follow Him. He did not dictate the promise based on gender; He did not give them descriptions of the type of fish they would seek, nor in which water to fish. Instead, He qualified the promise with, "Follow me" (v. 19).

God's ideal in creation is equality, mutuality, unity, and intimacy.

No task requires more patience than that of a fisherman.[1] Women, too, need patience in terms of walking out their own call and even as they read of women like Deborah and her three roles of prophetess, wife, and judge in the Book of Judges. Patience is required because they read about women of God walking out their call but are often unable to walk out their *own* call fully in the present day.

God's ideal in creation is equality, mutuality, unity, and intimacy. However, sin marred the original plan causing equality to be ignored, subordination imposed where he rules over her, unity severed, and

---

[1] Aimee Semple McPherson, "Fishers of Men," in *The Collected Sermons and Writings of Aimee Semple McPherson*, vol. 2 (North Charleston, SC: CreateSpace Independent Publishing, 2015), 9-16.

intimacy thwarted.[2] Egalitarianism was God's intent, yet sin created a hierarchy, and now the Church is in tension as God's plan continues to unfold.[3] Female leaders can be seen throughout the Old and New Testaments. Jesus included women even when it meant breaking social customs. Today, that call to women to follow Jesus remains and should not be interfered with. As Lisa Stephenson admonishes, "It would seem good to Holy Spirit not to burden women any further."[4]

The Problem

Leslie Stevens asserts that there is data to support that men and women do ministry differently, yet concerning authority, status, preaching, and social issues, there is no independent evidence that differences in style are inevitably defined by gender.[5] Female seminarians are more likely to accept ministerial positions at smaller congregations. As Barbara Finlay notes, perhaps women are more realistic about ministry opportunities to fulfill their calling.[6]

Althea Truman reports that a dual environment exists in which men seeking a leadership role receive a different response than women.[7]

---

[2] Deborah M. Gill and Barbara L. Cavaness, *God's Women: Then and Now* (Springfield, MO: Grace & Truth), 35-44.

[3] Gill and Cavaness, *God's Women*, 48.

[4] Lisa P. Stephenson, *Dismantling the Dualisms for American Pentecostal Women in Ministry: A Feminist-Pneumatological Approach*, vol. 9 of Global Pentecostal and Charismatic Studies (Leiden: Brill, 2012), 195.

[5] Lesley Stevens, "Different Voice/Different Voices: Anglican Women in Ministry," *262 Review of Religious Research* 30, no. 3 (1989): 262, https://doi.org/10.2307/3511511

[6] Barbara Finlay, "Do Men and Women Have Different Goals for Ministry? Evidence from Seminarians," *Sociology of Religion* 57, no. 3 (1996): 311-18, accessed November 10, 2020, http://www.jstor.org/stable/3712159.

[7] Althea W. Truman, "The Lived Experience of Leadership for Female Pastors in Religious Organizations" (Ph.D. diss, Capella University, Minneapolis, MN, 2010), Order No. 3418884, https://search.proquest.com/docview/753892386.

Although women serve in some of the highest government offices in the country, the Church continues to examine the Scriptures, searching for answers to the questions about women in ministry roles that continue to plague seminaries and conservative congregations across the country.[8]

The Purpose of This Study

The main purpose of this study is to investigate the experiences of senior female leadership within The Foursquare Church in an effort to analyze the representation of women in leadership positions. The project looks at the historical foundations of The Foursquare Church in the context of providing opportunity for women to serve in roles of authority; it assesses the experience of current senior female leaders in the institution to determine commonalities, themes, and patterns relative to the decline of representation of women in these positions.

> The Foursquare Church claims the egalitarian view, a concept this study will evaluate.

Three views exist regarding women's involvement in leadership within the church. The Foursquare Church claims the egalitarian view, a concept this study will evaluate. Matt Messner describes the three main views on female leadership in ministry as (1) egalitarianism—a theological view that both men and women are equally called and equipped by God to do to the work of the ministry at all leadership levels; (2) complementarianism—the view that males

---

[8] Gretchen E. Ziegenhals, "Women in Ministry: Beyond the Impasse," *The Center for Christian Ethics Baylor University*, 2009, Baylor University, accessed September 19, 2022, https://www.baylor.edu/content/services/document.php/98766.pdf.

and females are considered equal yet having different roles; and (3) egalitarian *but*—where statements in support of females in leadership are made but not supported and promises are made but go unfulfilled.[9]

Research Methodology and Significance

The Foursquare Church has experienced a decline in female senior leadership since the death of its founder. Therefore, this phenomenological study explores the experiences of five female senior leaders in The Foursquare Church. By analyzing participants' experiences, I anticipate gaining a more thorough understanding for the decline.

"Why are women underrepresented at the senior leadership level within The Foursquare Church?"

The guiding question throughout this research project is, "Why are women underrepresented at the senior leadership level within The Foursquare Church?" The secondary question is, "Are there commonalities in the experiences of each participant?" Thus, I will frame the direction of the study with the following questions:

1. What are the perceptions and experiences of senior female leadership in The Foursquare Church concerning opportunities or hindrances within the organization for women?

---

[9] Matt Messner, "Reasons Women Should Lead," CBE International, April 30, 2000, https://www.cbeinternational.org/resource/article/priscilla-papers-academic-journal/reasons-women-should-lead.

2. Are there commonalities in this study's five senior female leaders' experiences?

3. Is there any significance to the history of The Foursquare Church and its female founding visible today within the representation of female leaders? For example, do female leaders have the same accessibilities in ministry as their founder?

Studies of various denominations have been reported concerning female leadership representation. The results of several of these studies will be identified in the literature review of this project. Findings from Protestant and Catholic Churches' research of women in clergy roles and the hindrances they face are readily available. The reality of androcentric interpretation of Scripture, soft hypocrisy, and the ceilings that deter females from fulfilling the same call as their male counterparts have been studied.

This book focuses on The Foursquare Church, examining the intent of its founder, Sister Aimee, to determine whether her vision is still acceptable and followed.

This book focuses on The Foursquare Church, examining the intent of its founder, Sister Aimee, to determine whether her vision is still acceptable and followed. According to Jim Adams, The Foursquare Church's position on women in ministry is based on obedience to the Word of God, which requires inclusion of women as equal partners in ministry with men.[10] This egalitarian perspective of the

---

[10] Jim Adams, "Introduction," in *Women in Ministry Leadership: A Summary of the Biblical Position of the Foursquare Church Concerning God's Grace and a Woman's Potential under His Sovereignty and Call*, rev. ed., ed. Steve Schell (Los Angeles: Foursquare Media, 2021), 11.

interpretation of Scripture affirms the qualification for ministry is not based on gender.

Although research has previously been done on The Foursquare Church and women in leadership, none include an evaluation of experiences, perceptions, and opinions from female senior leaders. Therefore, this study fills a gap and addresses the following issues. First, with the participants holding senior leadership roles, their contribution from experience lends insight into any systemic issues that would not be evident without their seasoned experience. Second, the participants have successfully climbed uphill to their current assignments and bring knowledge of the hindrances they navigated to achieve these roles. Third, researchers have previously studied women in leadership ministry within The Foursquare Church, yet this study targets not those currently ascending but those already in position. Fourth, this study does not generalize female leadership but focuses on senior female leaders' experiences. Finally, the five participants bring to the study over one hundred years of faithful service to this egalitarian institution.

Limitations

This study is limited to five senior female leaders who serve in the United States, hold a Foursquare credential, and are in good standing with The Foursquare Church. These women will represent the 2,802 licensed women and the 132 female leaders in the denomination (at the time of this study).[11] The term *senior female leader* is defined as a woman who serves as a senior pastor, co-senior pastor (with a spouse), or in an executive leadership position.

---

[11] "This is Foursquare: Cabinet Report 2022," Foursquare Leader, accessed August 3, 2022, https://foursquare-leader.s3.us-east-1.amazonaws.com/about_us/business/2022-Cabinet-Report.pdf, 3.

These women will represent the 2,802
licensed women and the 132 female
leaders in the denomination (at
the time of this study).

The participants in this study are Caucasian and middle-class. Studies in search of similarities concerning opportunities and hindrances between various ethnicities of female leaders are suggested for further study. Also, a comparison of experiences between male and female senior leaders within The Foursquare Church is suggested.

Assumptions

In my research, I took for granted the following factors. First, the participants studied currently serve The Foursquare Church in a senior leadership role. Second, all information shared accurately reflects the participant's perceptions, understandings, opinions, and experiences while serving The Foursquare Church in a senior leadership capacity. Third, the participants answered the questions on the survey and in the interview openly and honestly.

Structure of this Book

This book is systematized into three Parts, which contain three chapters each. The final portion of the book (Part Four) contains appendix material, a glossary, select resources, and the full bibliography of my doctoral project.

Part One presents the biblical-theological study, providing a biblical-theological foundation for leadership, by examining the inclusion and acceptance of female leaders in a patriarchal culture. Following a brief overview of theological positions on female leadership, I also review Old and New Testament examples of key female leaders.

Part Two provides a literature review on current statistics and the experiences of women—including barriers they face to ministry opportunities—who are seeking or are in leadership positions. Although women successfully enter previously inaccessible careers, I examine gender gaps that still exist in specific occupations.[12] This Part takes a look at The Foursquare Church—at what *was*, what *is* today, and what *should be* for the future.

Part Three delineates the research methodology for my doctoral project. Using a qualitative methodology, I evaluated through interviews the experience of five female leaders in The Foursquare Church. This methodology proved integral to the project, as it allowed for examining phenomenon that each of the participants had encountered.[13] The final portion of Part Three contains my conclusions and recommendations to The Foursquare Church.

---

[12] T. H. Alaqahtani, "The Status of Women in Leadership," Research Gate, accessed July 6, 2022, https://www.researchgate.net/profile/Tahani-Alqahtani-2/publication/340514638_The_Status_of_Women_in_Leadership/links/60580b44458515e8345ff7bd/The-Status-of-Women-in-Leadership.pdf, 294-299.

[13] John W. Creswell and Cheryl N. Poth, *Qualitative Inquiry & Research Design: Choosing among Five Approaches*, 4th ed. (Los Angeles, CA: SAGE, 2018), 79.

PART ONE

For women or men questioning the authority or biblical right of female ministers, Part One examines the Scriptures. Following a brief overview of certain theological positions on female leadership, this section reviews Old and New Testament examples of key female leaders.

A theological challenge is that Jesus's maleness has been interpreted to mean that being male constitutes essential humanness while women were viewed as deficient humans.[1] This reasoning continues to plague women in the church as well as the home by defining and restricting their roles. Yet, the Bible is full of stories of female leaders, e.g., from Miriam (Exod. 15:20) to Rahab (Josh. 2) to Deborah (Judg. 4-5) to Huldah (2 Kgs. 22:14-20) to Esther (Esther 4:14). The Old Testament (OT) portion of Part One will review the examples of Deborah and Huldah.

Jesus engaged *her* in a theological discussion during a period when rabbis usually did not speak with women in public.

The New Testament (NT) presents the crucial roles of women such as Priscilla (Acts 18), Phoebe (Rom. 16), Lydia (Acts 16), Euodia and Syntyche (Phil. 4), Chloe (1 Cor. 1), and Junia (Rom. 16). The Samaritan woman was the first evangelist to convey the good news beyond Jewish culture (John 4:28). Jesus engaged *her* in a theological discussion during a period when rabbis usually did not speak with

---

[1] Stanley J. Grenz, *Theology for the Community of God* (Grand Rapids, MI: William B. Eerdmans Publishing Company, 1994), 288.

women in public.[2] Yet, just as other encounters with women, Jesus broke away from His fellow rabbis' prejudice (John 7:53-8:11; 11:17-40; Luke 7:36-50; 8:2-3; 10:38-42).[3] Jesus trusted the Samaritan woman with the most critical truth in Scripture. Her testimony provided the impetus for them to come to Jesus.[4] When two angels announced the good news of Jesus's resurrection, that message was again entrusted to women, who most in that cultural context considered unreliable messengers. The four Gospels record this truth (Matt. 28:1; Mark 16:1; Luke 24:10; John 20:1, 11).

Paul states in his letter to the Galatians
(3:28-29) that no hierarchy should exist
in the kingdom of God.

Paul states in his letter to the Galatians 3:28-29 that no hierarchy should exist in the kingdom of God: "There is neither Jew nor Greek; there is neither slave nor free; nor is there male and female, for you are all one in Christ Jesus. Now if you belong to Christ, then indeed you are Abraham's descendants, heirs according to the promise." This truth does not imply that one's sexual identity is lost at salvation; instead, it means that Jesus died as much for one sex as for the other.

The New Testament portion of Part One reviews the examples of Priscilla and Junia, discusses the pitfalls of andocentric interpretations of specific New Testament passages about women, and presents Jesus's response, respect, and release of women.

---

[2] Gerald Borchert, *John 1-11*, vol. 25A of *New American Commentary* (Nashville: Broadman & Holman, 2002), 202.
[3] Andreas J. Kostenberger, *John*, Baker Exegetical Commentary on the New Testament
(Grand Rapids, MI: Baker Academic, 2004), 159.
[4] Kostenberger, *John*, 164.

Chapter 1

Females and Female Leaders in the Old Testament

Introduction

A review of Genesis to Revelation reveals that God has strategically positioned women in critical roles. In the creation account, God values both men and women: "So God created humans in his image, in the image of God he created them; male and female he created them" (Gen. 1:27). Being made in His image produces likeness resulting in the creative nature evident in humans.

Evidence of women creating throughout Scripture mirrors the foundational statement of God in the Old Testament as Creator.

Evidence of women creating throughout Scripture mirrors the foundational statement of God in the Old Testament as Creator.[1] When it comes to trusting *man* with the future, God selected woman to be the carrier of all that is created in His image.

---

[1] Veli-Matti Kärkkäinen, *The Doctrine of God: A Global Introduction* (Grand Rapids, MI: Baker Academic, 2004), 21.

3

Overview of Select Scholarship
on Female Leadership

Complementarians (those with the view that men and women "complement" one another in their ordained roles)[2] consider the affirmation of women holding leadership roles within the church as unsound theology. However, several current biblical scholars affirm women as ministry leaders (e.g., F. F. Bruce, Gordon Fee, Ben Witherington, and Alan Johnson).

F. F. Bruce suggests that the world's culture should not influence the church; rather, the church should follow the instruction in Scripture regarding women in leadership roles.[3] He summarizes this well by stating,

> An appeal to first principles in our application of the New Testament might demand the recognition that when the Spirit, in his sovereign good pleasure, bestows varying gifts on individual believers, these gifts are intended to be exercised for the well-being of the whole church. If he [the Holy Spirit] manifestly withheld the gifts of teaching or leadership from Christian women, then we should accept that as evidence of his will (1 Cor 12:11). But experience shows that he bestows these and other gifts, with 'undistinguishing regard,' on men and women alike—not on all women, of course, nor yet on all men. That being so, it

---

[2] Complementarianism is, "A theological construct that assigns unique roles to men and women. Its teaching is rooted in an interpretation of the Bible that sees women and men as being created equal (Gen 1) but having different roles." Lori Harding, "Complementarianism Exists in Egalitarian Organizations and Churches Because of Patriarchy," CBE International, June 15, 2022, https://www.cbeinternational.org/resource/article/mutuality-blog-magazine/complementarianism-exists-egalitarian-organizations-and.

[3] F. F. Bruce, "Women in the Church: A Biblical Survey," *Christian Brethren Review* 33 (1982): 7-14; Theological Studies, accessed June 2, 2022, https://theologicalstudies.org.uk/pdf/cbr/women_bruce.pdf.

is unsatisfactory to rest with a halfway house in this issue of women's ministry, where they are allowed to pray and prophesy but not to teach or lead.[4]

Bruce's argument affirms that the church should follow the leading of the Spirit, who distributes gifts to both genders, and the gifts include leadership roles.

Gordon Fee, in *Discovering Biblical Equality*, argues that the church must release the workings and agenda of the Spirit so that it functions as God intended:

> It seems a sad commentary on the church and on its understanding of the Holy Spirit that "official" leadership and ministry is allowed to come from only one-half of the community of faith. The New Testament evidence is that the Holy Spirit is gender inclusive, gifting both men and women, and thus potentially setting the whole body free for all the parts to minister and in various ways to give leadership to the others. Thus, my issue in the end, is not a feminist agenda—advocacy of women in ministry. Rather, it is a Spirit agenda, a plea for the releasing of the Spirit from our strictures and structures so that the church might minister to itself and to the world more effectively.[5]

Fee suggests that the church has misunderstood the assignment of the Holy Spirit. Jesus knew that His disciples, both male and female, would need this power to witness to the ends of the world and excluded no one in the dispersal.

Ben Witherington shifts the conversation concerning women in leadership roles, yet he echoes egalitarianism in gift distribution. He

---

[4] Bruce, "Women in the Church," 7-14.
[5] Ronald W. Pierce, Rebecca Merrill Groothuis, and Gordon D. Fee, "The Priority of Spirit Gifting for Church Ministry," in *Discovering Biblical Equality: Complementarity without Hierarchy* (Downers Grove, IL: InterVarsity Press, 2005), 254.

notes that just as strengths within the home vary, so do the Spirit's assignment for individuals within church structure:

> [W]e need to keep steadily in mind that what determines or should determine the leadership structures in the church is not gender but rather gifts and graces of the Holy Spirit. The family of faith is not identical with the physical family, and gender is no determinant of roles in it. Gender of course does affect some roles in the Christian family, but that is irrelevant when it comes to the discussion of the leadership structure of the church.[6]

Witherington says the Spirit imparts without partiality and that the church will not function structurally and effectively without male and female contribution.

The family of faith is not identical with the physical family, and gender is not determinant of roles in it.
—Ben Witherington

Finally, Alan Johnson, editor of *How I Changed My Mind about Women in Leadership*, presents the compelling stories of several prominent evangelicals regarding how they changed their minds concerning women in ministry leadership. Dallas Willard writes in the introductory remarks to the book, "It is not the *rights* of women to occupy 'official' ministerial roles, nor their *equality* to men in those roles, that set the terms of their service to God and their neighbors. Instead, it is their *obligations* to do so—obligations that derive from

---

[6] Ben Witherington, "Why Arguments against Women in Ministry Aren't Biblical," Patheos, June 2, 2015, accessed July 12, 2022, https://www.patheos.com/blogs/bibleandculture/2015/06/02/why-arguments-against-women-in-ministry-arent-biblical/.

their human abilities empowered by divine gifting."[7] To exclude women from the ministries of teaching and preaching does incalculable damage to the church while profoundly affecting identity and worth on both sides.[8]

"It is not the *rights* of women to occupy
'official' ministerial roles, nor
their *equality* to men in those roles, that set
the terms of their service to God and their
neighbors. Instead, it is their
obligations to do so."
—Dallas Willard

In addition to these theological views on the intentional inclusion of female leaders in a patriarchal culture, the following two subsections review examples of inclusion within the Old and New Testaments.

Two Old Testament Female Leaders

Old Testament women lived in a patriarchal culture where men exercised unilateral authority over their household and society. Nevertheless, many of these women operated in nonpatriarchal tradition according to Gretchen Hull, and the biblical text commends them for their actions.[9] God uses a

---

[7] Alan F. Johnson, ed. *How I Changed My Mind about Women in Leadership: Compelling Stories from Prominent Evangelicals* (Grand Rapids, MI: Zondervan, 2010), vii.

[8] Johnson, ed., *How I Changed My Mind*, vii.

[9] Gretchen Gaebelein Hull, *Equal to Serve: Women and Men in the Church and Home* (NJ: Fleming H. Revell, 1987), 113. Gretchen Gaebelein Hull was instrumental in the founding of CBE (Christians for Biblical Equality) advancing the gospel by equipping Christians to use their God-given talents in leadership and service regardless of gender, ethnicity, or class.

woman—Deborah—to lead the nation of Israel to victory and another woman—Huldah—to introduce revival.

God uses a woman—Deborah—to lead the nation of Israel to victory and another woman—Huldah—to introduce revival.

The Book of Judges exhibits a repeated cycle[10] between the death of Israel's leader, Joshua, Israel's first king, Saul. Over and over the people of God plunge into moral compromise while worshipping false gods, become conquered militarily by neighboring tribes, then call out to God for help; then God raises up a judge to save His people from their enemies (Judg. 2:16, 18; 4:10; 14:24, 5:1-31). Amid this ancient civilization where patriarchal structures existed and men were accentuated, God groomed a woman as Israel's fourth judge in response to the people's cry.[11]

Deborah was the first judge described professionally as a prophet and decipherer of questions of law for the nation of Israel. Her authority transcended tribal divisions (Judg. 5).[12] As a prophet, she fulfilled the role of a prophet that the Apostle Paul describes in 1 Corinthians 14:3 as speaking "to other people for their upbuilding and encouragement and consolation." Deborah was also the wife of

---

She is a well-known prominent lecturer at evangelical seminaries and contributor to the *Study Bible for Women: The New Testament*, *Applying Scriptures*, and *Women, Authority and the Bible*.

[10] "And the people of Israel again did what was evil in the sight of the LORD after Ehud died. And the LORD sold them into the hand of Jabin king of Canaan, who reigned in Hazor. The commander of his army was Sisera, who lived in Harosheth-hagoyim. Then the people of Israel cried out to the LORD for help, for he had 900 chariots of iron and he oppressed the people of Israel for twenty years" (Judg. 4:1-3).

[11] Lawrence O. Richards, *The Teacher's Commentary* (Wheaton, IL: Victor Books, 1987), 182.

[12] Gill and Caveness, *God's Women Then and Now*, 49.

Lappidoth (Judg. 4:4). Although numerous titles are given to Deborah, first and foremost, she is a prophet (Judg. 4:4).[13] Barnabas Lindars refers to her role as a "war prophet."[14] Although the text gives no indication that God raised Deborah as the deliverer for His oppressed people, she is the one who God compelled to take the lead.

Deborah was the first judge described professionally as a prophet and decipherer of questions of law for the nation of Israel.

As a judge, Deborah would "sit under the palm of Deborah between Ramah and Bethel in the hill country of Ephraim, and the Israelites came up to her for judgment" (Judg. 4:5). The location where Deborah held court was centrally located between two cities, Ramah and Bethel, giving the entire nation of Israel accessibility.[15] A judge in Israel had more responsibilities than settling disputes among the people. Judges exercised all the functions of a governor, including executive and legislative authority and frequently military authority.[16] As judge and prophet, Deborah held offices most commonly held by men while simultaneously conforming to the role of a wife.[17]

Under Deborah's authority as prophet and judge, the text notes her summoning and commissioning Barak, general of the army, saying,

> "The Lord, the God of Israel, commands you, 'Position yourself at Mount Tabor, taking ten thousand from the tribe

---

[13] Daniel Isaac Block, *Judges, Ruth*, vol. 6 of *The New American Commentary* (Nashville: Broadman & Holman Publishers, 1999), 192.
[14] Barnabas Lindars, *Deborah's Song: Women in the Old Testament* (Manchester: J. Rylands University Library of Manchester, 1983), 183.
[15] Block, *Judges, Ruth*, 195.
[16] Richards, *The Teacher's Commentary*, 182-83.
[17] Trent Butler, ed., *Judges*, Word Biblical Commentary 8 (Nashville: Thomas Nelson, 2009), 94.

of Naphtali and the tribe of Zebulun. I will draw out Sisera, the general of Jabin's army, to meet you by the Wadi Kishon with his chariots and his troops, and I will give him into your hand.'" Barak said to her, "If you will go with me, I will go, but if you will not go with me, I will not go." And she said, "I will surely go with you; nevertheless, the road on which you are going will not lead to your glory, for the Lord will sell Sisera into the hand of a woman." Then Deborah got up and went with Barak to Kedesh (Judg. 4:6-9).

In this moment, Deborah's prophetic voice communicates God's response to the cry of the people, yet Deborah will ultimately not be the answer to that cry.

Barak trusted his life and the outcome to
one woman rather than to
ten thousand men.
—Trent Butler

Deborah leads Israel into combat while strategically plotting military strategy for the general, including the size of the army, the vantage point, and the moment of attack. Although having assurance from God of a victory, Barack responds, "If you will go with me, I will go, but if you will not go with me, I will not go" (Judg. 4:8). This statement appears to validate weakness; however, having the prophet's presence on the battlefield stimulated the troops, legitimizing the undertaking as divine.[18] Barak trusted his life and the outcome to one woman rather than to ten thousand men.[19] Deborah's promise to Barak robs him of the honor of the victory as she declares, "the Lord will sell Sisera into the hand of woman"

---

[18] John Peter Lange, et al., *A Commentary on the Holy Scriptures: Joshua* (Bellingham, WA: Logos Research Systems, 2008), 83.
[19] Butler, *Judges,* 99.

(Judg. 4:9). As Barak deploys his troops, God deploys the army of Sisera, Jabin's army commander, the overarching enemy.[20]

Barak, a man of faith, has respect for Deborah's gift and leadership (Heb. 11:32). Throughout the account of Judges 4, gender is never the focus—only the creativity of God. Deborah appears to experience more social and cultural freedom due to her profession, spiritual gifts, and favor. She is recognized as a confident leader, seen delegating assignments to God's people. Deborah holds the prophetic voice while Barak leads the army into battle, bringing the fulfillment of God's Word. God gives them the victory, "And the land had rest forty years" (Judg. 5:31).

Following the battle's success, Deborah and Barak sing praises to God for delivering His people to victory (Judg. 5:1-31). They describe, "when the people offer themselves willingly—bless the Lord!" (Judg. 5:1-2). In a male-centered culture, the people listened and followed God's spokesperson, a woman. In the song of Deborah and Barak, ten of the twelve tribes' participation is mentioned (Judg. 5:13-18). Five responded to the call: Ephraim, Benjamin, Zebulun, Issachar, and Naphtali, along with the western part of Manasseh. Four tribes (Reuben, Gilead, Dan, and Asher) and the other part of Manasseh did not join the battle. The fragmentation of Israel is evident as only a few tribes are represented in the battle.[21] Daniel Block contends that tribes may have been excused for noninvolvement because of distance or preoccupation with other duties; a strong element of rebuke is unmistakable in their absence (Judg. 5:17).[22]

In the song of Deborah and Barak, Meroz is mentioned with its city and inhabitants cursed (Judg. 5:23). The Lord did not require the

---

[20] Butler, *Judges*, 97.

[21] Butler, *Judges*, 96.

[22] Block, *Judges, Ruth,* 234.

assistance of Meroz to obtain victory. However, the decision between God and the kingdom of darkness cannot remain neutral as their silence maintains consent against God and His cause.[23] Several tribes, Reuben, Dan and Asher, chose to decline while Meroz, not one of the twelve tribes, chose indifference. Block contends that Meroz represents the Israelites who have taken their stand on the side of the Canaanites.[24] A. G. Auld supports the view that the people of Meroz were not Israelites since they are not mentioned among the tribes.[25] Phoebe Palmer, a prominent Methodist evangelist (1807-1874), exegetes the passage as an overt rejection to the leadership of women.[26] Regardless of Meroz's failure to support them, Deborah heard and spoke the words of the curse upon them.[27]

As the first female judge, prophet, wife, and designated with the title "Mother in Israel" (Judg. 5:7), Deborah, was not called by God to be a deliverer of His people but rather as a woman who sees the need and obeys the plan of God. Deborah, a wise woman, a warrior, and a leader of all people, bestows wisdom and leadership.[28] Because Deborah arose, "the land had rest for forty years" (Judg. 5:31).

The second woman in the Old Testament addressed in this portion of the chapter is Huldah. King Josiah of Judah, son of Amon and grandson of Manasseh, began ruling at eight years old following his

---

[23] Matthew Henry, *Matthew Henry's Commentary on the Whole Bible: Complete and Unabridged in One Volume* (Peabody, MA: Hendrickson, 1994), 338.
[24] Block, *Judges, Ruth,* 239
[25] A. G. Auld, *Joshua, Judges, Ruth: The Daily Study Bible Series* (Philadelphia: Westminster, 1984), 159.
[26] Phoebe Palmer, *Promise of the Father; or, A Neglected Specialty of the Last Days, Addressed to the Clergy and Laity of All Christian Communities* (1859; repr., Salem: Schmul Publishers, 1981), 2.
[27] Carl Friedrich Keil and Franz Delitzsch, *Joshua, Judges, Ruth, 1 & 2 Samuel,* vol. 2 of *Commentary on the Old Testament* (Peabody, MA: Hendrickson, 1996), 234.
[28] James Clark-Soles, *Interpretation Resource for the Use of Scripture in the Church: Women in the Bible* (Louisville, KY: Westminster John Knox Press, 2020), 118.

father's death, and he reigned thirty-one years in Jerusalem (2 Kings 22:1). According to the biblical narrative, he "did what was right in the eyes of the LORD and walked in all the ways of David, his father" (2 Kings 22:2). In the eighteenth year of Josiah's reign, the Jerusalem Temple renovations took place (2 Kings 22:3-6). King Josiah sent Shaphan, secretary to the house of the Lord to take care of financial business (2 Kings 22:3).

> Although Jeremiah was a respected prophet already having five years of experience during King Josiah's reign, Jeremiah was not the prophet sought after.

Upon arrival, Hilkiah, the high priest, says to Shaphan the secretary, "I have found the Book of the Law[29] in the house of the Lord (2 Kings 22:8). The Book was given to Shaphan and returned to King Josiah, where it was read (2 Kings 22:8-10). According to the account in this chapter,

> When the king heard the words of the book of the law, he tore his clothes. Then the king commanded the priest Hilkiah, Ahikam son of Shaphan, Achbor son of Micaiah, Shaphan the secretary, and the king's servant Asaiah, saying, "Go, inquire of the Lord for me, for the people, and for all Judah, concerning the words of this book that has been found, for great is the wrath of the Lord that is kindled against us, because our ancestors did not obey the words of this book to do according to all that is written concerning us" (2 Kings 22:11-13).

---

[29] The scroll has been agreed upon by scholarly consensus to be the Book of Deuteronomy; see Robert Alter, "The Hebrew Bible: A Translation with Commentary Prophets," in *The Hebrew Bible: A Translation with Commentary Prophets* (New York: W.W. Norton & Company, 2019), 601.

King Josiah was fearful of the content within the scroll and sought out someone with prophetic gifting to investigate whether the punishment due them could be averted.

After Huldah interprets the scroll, Josiah replies to the mercy of God.

Jeremiah had served as one of God's prophets from the days of Josiah through the reigns of Judah's last four kings (Jehoahaz, Jehoiakim, Jehoiachin and Zedekiah). He continued during Jerusalem's destruction by the Babylonians in 586 BC (Jer. 1:3; 52:7-11). Although Jeremiah was a respected prophet already having five years of experience during King Josiah's reign, Jeremiah was not the prophet sought after. Zephaniah, also a prophet in the day of Josiah, king of Judah, was not sought. The men made their way to God's representative, a woman, a prophet named Huldah, wife of Shallum (2 Kings 22:14). Huldah is the only female prophet mentioned in the Book of Kings. The men, a royal delegation sent by the king, accept her full authority.[30] They approach Huldah, and she interprets God's Word to them about the fact of and reasons for the coming disaster as well as God's acceptance of and reward for humility and repentance (2 Kings 22:16-20). The idolatry of the people would lead to great consequences. However, because of Josiah's humility and grief over the nation's sin, he would die in peace prior to the judgment of the people.

Although Jeremiah was a respected prophet already having five years of experience during King Josiah's reign, Jeremiah was not the prophet sought after.

---

[30] Alter, "The Hebrew Bible," 601.

After Huldah interprets the scroll, Josiah replies to the mercy of God. He calls the nation of Israel to repentance, destroys the altars to false gods, encourages them to follow the Lord and keep His commandments, and removes all idolatry. As a result, the people pledge themselves to the covenant (2 Kings 23:1-3). The obedience of Huldah, trusted by God and by man, was responsible for the most significant spiritual revival in Israel's history (2 Kings 22:11-23:25).

Chapter 2

Females and Female Leaders in the New Testament

Two New Testament Female Leaders

Women hold various key leadership roles while leading men and co-leading with men throughout the New Testament. Terran Williams suggests that while complementarian scholars focus on Adam being first, Jesus often puts women first, affirming, including, and releasing them into all roles of ministry leadership.[1] Two women, Junia and Priscilla, hold key roles in the New Testament as church planters, theologians, leaders, and advancers of the Kingdom.

Junia

The first woman addressed here is Junia. Jesus appointed and sent out the Twelve to preach, heal the sick, and cast out demons—naming them apostles (Mark 3:14-15). Paul also refers to himself as an apostle: "Paul an apostle—sent neither by human commission nor from human authorities but through Jesus Christ and God the Father, who raised him from the dead—" (Gal 1:1), yet he is not listed among the Twelve. There are other apostles in Scripture not

---

[1] Terran Williams, *How God Sees Women: The End of Patriarchy* (Cape Town South Africa: The Spiritual Bakery Publications, 2022), 223. Terran Williams is a CBE (Christians for Biblical Equality) contributor focusing on the crises within complementarianism assisting in navigating the arguments against the inclusion of women. He has a forward-looking vision for mutualism.

among the originals: Matthias (Acts 1:26), Barnabas (Acts 14:14), Andronicus and Junia (Rom. 16:7), Titus and his unnamed companion (2 Cor. 8:23), James the Lord's brother (Gal. 1:19), and Epaphroditus (Phil. 2:25).[2]

Paul introduces Andronicus and Junia as "my fellow Israelites who were in prison with me" in the Book of Romans (Rom. 16:7). He mentions that they are prominent among the apostles and were in Christ before him (Rom. 16:7). Paul knew them and acknowledged them as "prominent among the apostles" (Rom. 16:7). Andronicus and Junia are introduced as a twosome, lending interpreters to often assume the two were married. However, the text is unclear on this subject.

Lively debate exists among scholars concerning two interpretive issues in Romans 16:7: the name Junia and the relationship of Junia and Andronicus in apostolic circles. The phrase in question regarding the association of Junia and Andronicus is "*episēmoi en tois apostolois.*" The standard NT lexicon provides one meaning, "outstanding among the apostles."[3] New Testament Scholar J. B. Lightfoot (1828-1889) agrees that the natural way to translate *episēmoi en tois apostolois* is "regarded as apostles."[4] NT scholar F. F. Bruce (1910-1990), adds that they are "well known to the apostles," but they were "notable members of the apostolic circle."[5] Virtually all English translations of the Bible have solidified *episēmoi en tois*

---

[2] Dennis J. Preato, "Junia, a Female Apostle: An Examination of the Historical Record," CBE International, April 25, 2019, accessed June 2, 2020, https://www.cbeinternational.org/resource/article/priscilla-papers-academic-journal/junia-female-apostle-examination-historical.
[3] "BDAG 378," CBE International, accessed June 2, 2022, https://www.cbeinternational.org/.
[4] Walter Schmithals, *The Office of Apostle in the Early Church*, trans. John E Steely (New York: Abingdon, 1969), 62.
[5] F. F. Bruce, *Paul: Apostle of the Heart Set Free* (Grand Rapids: Eerdmans, 1981), 298, 388.

apostolois as "among the apostles," meaning that both Junia and Andronicus were apostles.[6]

Virtually all English translations of the Bible have solidified *episēmoi en tois apostolois* as "among the apostles," meaning that both Junia and Andronicus were apostles.
—Dennis J. Preato

Horace Bushnell, a leading U.S. theologian of the nineteenth century, shared an account from 1869 where an influential American theologian and minister wrote that women were not created nor called to govern, nor should they have the right to vote; he predicted: "If women started voting, their brains would swell, and they would eventually lose their femininity and morals."[7] Other voices argued that mothers should stay in their places doing what God intended for them and that their husbands would vote for them. These prejudices against women to disallow their voting privileges likely contributed to the bias reflected in various biblical translations modifying the gender of *Iounian* (Junia) from female to male—without textual support.[8] The magnitude of patriarchal influence and an androcentric interpretation of Scripture continues to impact gender equality.

---

[6] Preato, *Junia, a Female Apostle.*
[7] Horace Bushnell, "Women's Suffrage: The Reform against Nature: Bushnell, Horace, 1802-1876: Free Download, Borrow, and Streaming Bushnell," Internet Archive (New York: Scribner, January 1, 1869), https://archive.org/details/womenssuffragere00bushrich. Horace Bushnell (1802-1876) attended Yale where he first studied law, then later theology. Over the course of his life, Bushnell authored a dozen books and gained renoun as a minister, theologian, and civic leader.
[8] Preato, *Junia, a Female Apostle.*

Before the thirteenth century, biblical commentators unanimously agreed that Junia was a female name.

The magnitude of patriarchal influence and an androcentric interpretation of Scripture continues to impact gender equality.

Preato reports that mainstream translations from the late 1300s through the 1800s agree with the female name. By the early twentieth-century, Weymouth (1903), Montgomery NT (1924), Riveduta (1927), Lams Bible (1933), and Bible in Basic English (1949) were also in agreement. By the later twentieth-century other versions presenting Junia as a woman include: CJB, GNT, GW, HCSB, ISV, KJ21, NCV, NIRV, NIVUK, NLT, NKJV, NRSV, NRSVA, NRSVACE, NRSVCE, REB, TMB, WE; since 2000, at least thirty new translations or revisions translate Iounian as Junia.[9]

Eldon Epp claims, "It was the thirteenth edition of the Nestle text and somewhat earlier with English translations, [that] the female Junia becomes the male Junias and remained until the 1970s when once again Junia enters the picture."[10] Since the 1970s, several biblical translations have adjusted the name from male to female. Epp suggests the tension existing in interpreting male or female versions of the name Junia within the text is based upon the location of the accent mark.[11] However, in Scribes and Scholars, the authors state, "The system of accentuation … was not invented until the Hellenistic period, and for a long time after its invention it was not universally used; here again it is not until the early middle ages that

---

[9] Preato, *Junia, a Female Apostle.*
[10] Eldon Jay Epp, *Junia: The First Woman Apostle* (Minneapolis: Fortress, 2005), 22.
[11] Epp, *Junia,* 22.

the writing of accents becomes normal practice."[12] With the additional contribution from Reynolds and Wilson, the change from male to female was founded on something other than the transcription of the original Greek manuscript.

Greek Church Father John Chrysostom (c. AD 347-407), who served as Archbishop of Constantinople, affirms Junia as a female and is particularly convincing considering his misogynistic view.[13] Chrysostom penned the following quote in the late 300s/early 400s while Junia was recognized as female apostle in the Early Church, stating,

> Greet Andronicus and Junia…who are outstanding among the apostles: To be an apostle is something great. But to be outstanding among the apostles—just think what a wonderful song of praise that is! They were outstanding on the basis of their works and virtuous actions. Indeed, how great the wisdom of this woman must have been that she was even deemed worthy of the title of apostle. (In ep. Ad Romanos 31:2; PG 60.669-670).[14]

In the following century, Theodoret, Bishop of Cyrrhus, says, "Then to be called 'of note' not only among the disciples but also among the teachers, and not just among the teachers but even among the apostles…"[15] Origen of Alexandria (AD 185-254), theologian and

---

[12] Leighton Durham Reynolds and Nigel Guy Wilson, *Scribes and Scholars: A Guide to the Transmission of Greek and Latin Literature*, 3rd ed. (Oxford: Clarendon Press, 1991), 4.
[13] Leonard J. Swidler, *Biblical Affirmations of Women* (Philadelphia: The Westminster Press, 1979), 299.
[14] Bernadette Brooten, "'Junia … Outstanding among the Apostles' (Romans 16:7) (1)," Women Priests, June 29, 2021, https://womenpriests.org/articles-books/brooten-junia-outstanding-among-the-apostles-romans-167-1.
[15] Linda Belleville et al., "Ιουνιαν … Επισημοι Εν Τοις Αποστολοις: A Re-Examination of Romans 16.7 in Light of Primary Source Materials," BELLEVILLE, LINDA | download, 2005, https://ur.booksc.me/book/38987095/500e1b.

biblical commentator, also agreed that the name Junia was female despite his previous misogynistic statements.[16]

Epp submits seven convincing motivations that "Junia," the feminine name, is the most natural reading of Romans 16:7 and must be considered in the interpretation:

(a) Junia was a common roman name for either noble members of the gens Junia (the clan of Junia) or for freed slaves of the gens (or their descendants)—with the freed slaves more numerous than the nobles. (b) Junia was how the term was understood whenever discussed by ancient Christian writers of late antiquity "without exception." (c) Junia was the reading of Greek New Testaments from Erasmus in 1516 to Erwin Nestle's edition of 1927 (with the exception of Alford in 1852) and during that period no alternate reading appears to have been in any apparatus (except Weymouth [1892]). (d) All early extant translations (Old Latin, Vulgate, Sahidic and Bohairic Coptic and Syriac versions) without exception transcribe the name in what can be taken as a feminine form: none gives any positive sign that a masculine name is being transcribed. (e) The feminine Junia is how Romans 16:7 was read in English translations of the New Testament from Tyndale (1526/1534) almost without exception until the last quarter of the nineteenth century. (f) Neither of the alleged masculine forms of the name Junias has been found anywhere. (g) The hypothesis of Junias as a contracted name has serious problems.[17]

---

[16] Brooten, "'Junia . . . Outstanding among the Apostles' (Romans 16:7) (1)."

[17] Epp, *Junia: The First Woman Apostle*, 23. Regarding item (c), Epp cites W. F. Moulton and A. S. Geden, *A Concordance to the Greek Testament* (Edinburgh: T & T Clark, 1897). Regarding item (d), Epp cites John Thorley, *Junia, A Woman Apostle* (Leiden: E. J. Brill, 1996), 20.

Mead notes six points to this conversation in his project, "Who Killed Junia?" with the following:

> (1) When Constantine organized the early church he did so with Roman eyes and attitudes. Men ruled Roman society so he assumed that was the only proper way to rule the church, ignoring the fact that there is no male or female, Jew or Greek, slave or free in the new community of faith. He ignored the daughters of Philip, Dorcas/Tabitha, Junia, Julia, a slew of Marys, Priscilla, Phoebe, and more. (2) Then came Giles and Pope Boniface who stripped nuns of their powers and authority in the church, shoving them into a cloistered, separate existence. (3) Martin Luther launched the Reformation but he was more anti-women than most priests of his day. He considered them nothing more than child-bearers, incubators for men's seed. (4) Victorian England made male and female roles even more rigid and defined by "decency" and "acceptable standards." (5) The American South enthusiastically championed those roles and attitudes. They became part of American fundamentalism and the text was changed to match the attitude of the times. (6) In the 1980s, when the New International Version announced a translation with gender-accurate language, conservative evangelicals rebelled. Articles were written, sermons preached, and threats were made. The plan was abandoned and it was published only in Europe. It wasn't until 2011 that the NIV was republished in the U.S., not because the text didn't support it, but because of opposition from the prevailing male culture of the church. It isn't pretty … but it's true.[18]

---

[18] Patrick Mead, "Who 'Killed' Junia? Part One," The Junia Project, May 2, 2014, accessed July 15, 2022, https://juniaproject.com/who-killed-junia-part-one/; See also Mead, "Who 'Killed' Junia? Part Two."

After examining the two issues of interpretation regarding Junia from Romans 16:7, it must be concluded that linguistic and historical evidence overwhelmingly support Junia as a female name and that she was the first and only woman termed apostle in the canonical writings.[19]

> Although surrounded by a patriarchal culture, Junia did not remain silent.

Junia was a type-two apostle, not one of the original Twelve, but a member of the broader circle of apostles, including Paul, Barnabas, and James, all sent by Jesus.[20] Although surrounded by a patriarchal culture, Junia did not remain silent. Junia led men and taught all people the gospel of Jesus Christ.

Priscilla

The second key woman in the New Testament addressed here is Priscilla. Mentioned alongside her husband, Aquila, at least six times in the New Testament, Priscilla is one of the most prominent leaders in the Pauline trajectory of Christianity. She appears in the Pauline letters, the Deutero-Paulines, and the Book of Acts. This may seem insignificant to the modern reader, but in ancient patriarchal literature, the woman's name is rarely mentioned.[21] C. K. Barrett suggests that the mention of Priscilla so frequently by name showed her as undoubtedly outstanding in her own right; Aquila's uniqueness in the NT relates to his never being named without his

---

[19] Epp, *Junia*, 29.
[20] Kroeger and Kroeger, *Suffer Not a Woman*, 241.
[21] Terran Williams, "Resolving Five Complementarian Protests to Priscilla the Pastor-Teacher," CBE International, June 5, 2022, accessed July 6, 2022, https://www.cbeinternational.org/resource/article/mutuality-blog-magazine/resolving-five-complementarian-protests-priscilla-pastor.

wife.[22] Both Paul and Luke list Priscilla first in their writings (Acts 18:2-3, 18-19, 26; Rom. 16:3-4; 1 Cor. 16:19; 2 Tim. 4:19). The appeal of this account is the evidence of Priscilla leading women and also effectively leading in partnership with her husband. Priscilla leads without any awareness of divine rules disallowing her to teach or lead men.

> Priscilla is one of the most prominent
> leaders in the Pauline trajectory
> of Christianity.

The Apostle Paul refers to Priscilla and Aquila, Urbanus (Rom. 16:9), Timothy (Rom. 16:21), Titus (2 Cor. 8:23), Clement (Phil. 4:3), and Philemon (Philem 1) as "coworkers" and asks that Christians be subject to these.[23] Referring to others as "coworkers" was no mention that would have been unnoticed in the first century. Paul refers to twenty-five people in one chapter (Rom. 16) while praising seven women and five men pointing out that they were crucial to the success of his work and the accomplishments with the church.[24] Paul reports living and laboring with Priscilla and Aquila in Corinth (Acts 18:2) and in Ephesus (Acts 18:19; 20:34). The couple maintained a church inside their home wherever they lived (Acts 18:2, 26; Rom. 16:3-5; 1 Cor. 16:19; 2 Tim. 4:19). Without these two disciples [Priscilla and Aquila], the church might not have turned out as it did. According to 1 Corinthians, Paul arrived in Corinth "in weakness and in fear and in much trembling," and the two welcomed him in while facilitating his missionary activities (1 Cor. 2:3).

---

[22] C. K. Barrett, *Acts 15-28,* vol. 2 of *International Critical Commentary* (T & T Clark, London: T & T Clark, 1998), 861.

[23] James Clark-Soles, *Interpretation Resource for the Use of Scripture in the Church Women in the Bible* (Louisville: Westminster John Knox Press, 2020), 254.

[24] Mead, "Who 'Killed' Junia? Part Two."

Priscilla was a multi-talented woman. According to Acts 18:1-3, she and her husband, Aquila, were tentmakers. As a businesswoman, Priscilla labored alongside her husband. After leaving Rome under the edict of Claudius that expelled all Jews from Rome, they arrived in Corinth, where they met Paul, also a tentmaker, and the three worked and ministered together.

Without these two disciples [Priscilla and Aquila], the church might not have turned out as it did.

Priscilla and Aquila accompanied Paul to Syria and then to Ephesus, where they remained while he continued his journey (Acts 18:18-19). While in Ephesus, they were introduced to an Alexandrian Jew named Apollos. Priscilla's Christianity was solid; she demonstrated her faith in that she and her husband corrected and instructed Apollos, the learned and eloquent teacher. They "explained the Way of God to him more accurately" (Acts 18:24-26). As one faithfully arguing Jesus as Messiah to the Jews in a public forum, Apollos was successful in communicating why Jesus was the Messiah, but he still lacked understanding of the significance of the resurrection of Jesus and how it fulfilled the requirements of the Messiah. When the two heard Apollos' teaching, they intervened discreetly, educating him on the rest of the lesson. Apollos accepted the teaching, demonstrating a relationship between the three. Following this, the Early Church began referring to Priscilla as "a teacher of teachers."[25] Chrysostom, although known for making many statements against women, declares: "Priscilla took Apollos, an eloquent man and mighty in the Scriptures, but knowing only the baptism of John; and she instructed him in the way of the Lord and made him a teacher

---

[25] Kroeger and Kroeger, *Suffer Not a Woman*, 55.

brought to completion (Acts 18:24-25)."[26] This affirmation by Chrysostom, a man contributing to the erosion concerning the power of women, amplifies the interpretation of Priscilla's role.

Priscilla, also referred to as Prisca, is briefly introduced in Acts 18, yet more times than not in NT passages, she is listed first in the accounts. When New Testament writers consistently list someone first, it is typically a testament to their ministry prominence. Although Priscilla ministers alongside her husband, Aquila, this is not a representation of the complementarian's view of co-pastoring where the male is the pastor-teacher; rather, in this account, it appears that the pastor-teacher is Priscilla. Priscilla causes great distress and manufactures doubt to the complementarian interpretation of 1 Timothy 2:12 as she is clearly a female pastor-teacher in the Early Church.

God's intention from the beginning, evidenced in Scripture, was inclusion.

God's intention from the beginning, evidenced in Scripture, was inclusion. The Old and New Testaments find examples of women leading and serving in critical roles. Selected scholars and Church Fathers have affirmed women's place in leadership within the church, yet women continue to struggle to take their place as a result of biblical interpretation.

---

[26] Catherine Clark Kroeger, "John Chrysostom's First Homily on the Greeting to Priscilla and Aquila," CBE International, July 30, 1991, accessed July 12, 2022, https://www.cbeinternational.org/resource/article/priscilla-papers-academic-journal/john-chrysostoms-first-homily-greeting-priscilla.

Chapter 3

New Testament Passages on Women in Leadership

It is interesting to note that in the New Testament, women are found in places where expected and also in places where they are not. For example, women were not listed among the twelve disciples, at the transfiguration, the last supper, or at the Garden of Gethsemane. In the feeding of the 5,000 and 4,000, only men are counted (e.g., Matt. 14:13-21; 15:29-39) because women and children were lesser citizens. However, amid this patristic culture, God places women in leadership roles.

This study will analyze if this denomination [The Foursquare Church] maintains consistency in interpreting Scripture about women in leadership.

This chapter reviews women in leadership roles in the New Testament—but first, a comment on the authority of the Bible. The Foursquare Church affirms the Bible as the "true, immutable, steadfast, and unchangeable" word of God.[1] Then there needs to be consistency in interpretation. This study will analyze if this

---

[1] "Declaration of Faith Compiled by Aimee Semple McPherson," Foursquare, accessed January 5, 2023, https://foursquare-org.s3.amazonaws.com/assets/Declaration_of_Faith.pdf.

denomination [The Foursquare Church] maintains consistency in interpreting Scripture about women in leadership.

The Bible consists of absolute truths and relative statements.

When considering "male-female mutualism,"[2] as the Bible demonstrates in the creation account (Gen. 2-3)—and exhibited by various female leaders serving in key roles within Scripture—tension exists today concerning the interpretation of specific passages concerning women in church leadership.

The Bible consists of absolute truths and relative statements. Absolute truths mean "true" at all times and relative statements being "linked" by a specific time, place, and situation. This inconsistency in interpretation has led to manufactured hierarchy in opposition to a God-ordained structure.[3]

Peter's Announcement
(Acts 2:14-21)

In obedience to Jesus's command, the disciples go to Jerusalem to wait for the promise of the coming of the Holy Spirit (Acts 1:4-5, 13-15). In Acts 2, as the believers gather in unity, the Spirit anoints the men and women with the gift of tongues (Acts 2:1-4). The crowd hears the sound of wind, sees the tongues of fire on their heads, and listen to the followers of Jesus glorify God in the language of each of Jerusalem visitors, and are in wonder. Peter responds to the phenomenon by declaring that this is manifestation of fulfilling the

---

[2] Williams, *How God Sees Women*, 22.

[3] The Foursquare Church confronts these passages, bringing clarity and solidifying its posture concerning women in ministry leadership. Their stance is a matter of obedience to Scripture rather than any compromise in support of its female founder.

prophecy of Joel, "Then afterward I will pour out my spirit on all flesh; your sons and your daughters shall prophesy, your old men shall dream dreams, and your young men shall see visions" (Joel 2:28). If Peter is being Spirit-led in his proclamation of this Old Testament prophet, then the Holy Spirit is given without discrimination, and the new community of believers begins without gender barriers.

The inclusion of women in Joel 2:28 and throughout the Scriptures reflects the divine intent for women to have the opportunity to lead.

Prophecy is God speaking through human vessels, and the one prophesying is exercising spiritual authority and this gift (as we see in Acts) is given to men and women. The inclusion of women in Joel 2:28 and throughout the Scriptures reflects the divine intent for women to have the opportunity to lead. These two passages, Joel 2:28-31 and Acts 2:14-21, present a challenge for those who believe Paul forbade women to minister in gatherings with men. If accurate, then the inference is that Paul contradicts Peter's proclamation about the fulfillment of Joel's prophecy. However, as will be evident in the following section, Paul agrees with Peter that the promised era had arrived and that *all* those made in God's image (Gen. 1:26-27) were empowered for ministry. As Melissa Archer notes, "This new breath of the Spirit thus revives the egalitarian intent for humanity created in the *imago Dei* ... lost in the Fall of humanity (see Gen. 3), and restored in *imago Christi* (Gal. 3:28)."[4] However, how the Spirit's

---

[4] Melissa Archer, "Women in Ministry: A Pentecostal Reading of New Testament Texts," in *Women in Pentecostal and Charismatic Ministry: Informing a Dialogue on Gender, Church, and Ministry*, ed. Margaret English de Alminana and Lois E. Olena, vol. 21 of Global Pentecostal and Charismatic Studies (Leiden: Brill, 2017), 37-38.

outpouring at Pentecost would play out in the early church and throughout Church history would not take place without controversy. To examine this idea, the subject turns to the teachings of Paul.

Teachings of Paul

Paul is believed to be responsible for penning several passages that continue to challenge egalitarianism, and this section considers these passages. These are the same Scriptures The Foursquare Church addresses in their doctrinal handbook concerning women in ministry leadership.[5] Considering these passages, this section aims to examine the beliefs and practices of The Foursquare Church concerning female senior leadership to determine the representation, hindrances, and appointments available to female leaders of The Foursquare Church.

In his first letter to the Corinthian Church Paul discusses "male headship" (i.e., in the context of covering the head while praying or prophesying) citing the creation account as validation for this admonition. However, the creation account does not infer a hierarchy. According to Genesis 1:26-27, male and female are made in the image of God to participate in His assignments without role distinctions, and no structure of authority between the two is mentioned, until sin enters.

In Bonnie Dwyer's article on headship, she describes Gerry Chudleigh's explanation of "headship theology" as a new way of using the Bible to support old-fashioned patriarchalism while referring to it as complementarianism; Chudleigh claims that "headship theology" was further developed by Evangelical Calvinists

---

[5] Jim Adams et al., *Women in Ministry Leadership: A Summary of the Biblical Position of the Foursquare Church Concerning God's Grace and a Woman's Potential under His Sovereignty and Call* (Los Angeles: Foursquare Media, 2021), 11-44.

Wayne Grudem, James B. Hurley, and John Piper in response to feminism within the Church.[6] Chudleigh reports that four specific occurrences in the early 1970s prompted this fear. First, the Equal Rights Amendment, Title IX, which makes it illegal for schools to spend more money on the educational programs for men then what it spends on the same programs for women. Second, Roe v. Wade giving women the right to elective abortions. Third, the Merikay Silver/Lorna Tobler lawsuit against Pacific Press making a permanent impact upon the church requiring equal pay of women and men. Fourth, a ten-year controversy surrounding the ordination of Seventh-Day Adventist Women, the Mohaven study. The church's response to perceived threats of women's rights was a "biblical headship theology calling women to submission."[7] This

---

[6] Bonnie Dwyer, "Gerry Chudleigh Explains the History of Headship Theology," Spectrum Magazine, May 2, 2014, accessed July 12, 2022, https://spectrummagazine.org/article/bonnie-dwyer/2014/05/02/gerry-chudleigh-explains-history-headship-theology. Gerry Chudleigh was the communications director for the Pacific Union Conference, the Seventh-day Adventist Church. He answered questions before the Theology of Ordination Study committee *about female ordination and was well-versed in Adventist history related to the topic, as the denomination continued to wrestle with ordaining women. Chudleigh focuses on the difference between headship theology and patriarchy. He claims that* the old arguments for patriarchalism often claimed that women were inferior to men, and they focused on specific biblical instructions, like women keeping silent in church and never teaching men. Those interpretations of the Bible have never proven acceptable to Adventists, partly because they contrast with the leadership role of Ellen White (one of the founders of the Seventh Day Adventist Church in 1863). See primary reference to Chudleigh here: "A Historic Look at the Seventh Day Adventist Church," Seventh-day Adventist Church, accessed August 8, 2022, https://www.adventist.org/who-are-seventh-day-adventists/history-of-seventh-day-adventists/. The new headship advocates try hard to maintain that women are as intelligent, capable and valuable as men; God has just assigned them different roles than men. Many critics have pointed out, though, that the traditional demeaning of women is still implied. Because the new headship theology focuses on a "principle" of men leading and women submitting, it is not limited by what the Bible actually says.

[7] Dwyer, "Gerry Chudleigh Explains."

response was initiated with the interpretation of one Greek word, *head*.

David Scholer claims that those who oppose equal partnership of males and females in ministry uniformly argue that the term "head" in the English language means "authority," "leader or master," where men are to have authority over women and should conform to the *structure* God intended.[8] Others argue that the term "head" means "source" or "origin," referring to the creation account having nothing to do with hierarchy but rather a chronological reference that Adam precedes Eve in the creation.[9] As significant as the term "head" appears in this passage, Paul ultimately affirms the full participation of males and females in prayer and prophecy, which he considers the most crucial function for the building up and growth of the church (1 Cor 14). Therefore, I argue that neither this passage nor any another NT text supports the idea of subordination of women to men.

---

[8] David M. Scholer, *Male Headship: God's Intention or Man's Invention* (Berkeley: WATCHword, 1988), 3-4, 7. David Scholer was an American Baptist Bible Scholar and advocate for women in ministry. He was a New Testament professor at Fuller Theological Seminary (1994-2008) and joined the Evangelical Women's Caucus (EWC) in the 1970s. For thirty-six years at four seminaries he taught "Women and Ministry in the New Testament and the Church Today," explaining that a careful reading of the Gospels and the letters of Paul demands full inclusion of women in church leadership. He personally mentored many female students and friends as they became pastors.

[9] Deborah Gill and Barbara Cavaness describe the Garden of Eden as a place of innocence where God demonstrates His ideal for the male-female relationship. In Genesis 1:27 God created man in His own image. The term "man" in this passage does not represent a male person but rather male and female, constituting humanity. This passage demonstrates that male and female are created equally in God's image. Gill and Cavaness, *God's Women Then and Now*, 36.

Craig Keener submits that Paul addresses four main arguments in 1 Corinthians.[10] For the purpose of this book, two of those arguments will be studied. First, in discussing the idea of the husband as the head (1 Cor. 11:3-6), Keener supports Scholer's theory that the term "head" is not a common meaning for "leader" in the Greek language.[11] As Gordon Fee mentions, "the only "authority" in this passages is the woman's own authority (1 Cor. 11:10), and 11:11-12 "explicitly qualify vs 8-9 so that they will not be understood hierarchically.""[12] Keener aligns with other scholars in that "head" means "source" in this passage as woman was derived from man (1 Cor. 11:8).[13] There are no indications in this passage of the husband's "authority; " instead, as Keener notes, Paul is addressing a specific audience of women and that the importance of head covering has less to do with apparel than it does with its effects.

Second, regarding the creation order to which Paul references (1 Cor. 11:7-12), Keener states that because woman was taken from man, she reflects man's image and ought to cover that image in worship so as not to distract observers' attention to God's image.[14] He continues: "Paul is not unaware that woman and man together make up God's image and he [Paul] references this elsewhere that all believers are being conformed into the image of Christ."[15] Keener recapitulates this idea by stating, "Women and men are each derived from the other in some sense, and the ultimate source or head of

---

[10] Craig S. Keener, *Paul, Women & Wives: Marriage and Women's Ministry in the Letters of Paul* (Peabody, MA: Hendrickson, 2004), 34-38.

[11] Keener, *Paul, Women & Wives*, 32.

[12] Gordon Fee, *The First Epistle to the Corinthians* (Grand Rapids, MI: Eerdmans Publishing Company, 1987), 530.

[13] E.g., Fee, *First Epistle to the Corinthians*, 503-04.

[14] W. H. Leslie, "The Concept of Woman in the Pauline Corpus in Light of the Social and Religious Environment of the First Century" (Ph.D. diss., Northwestern University, 1976), 107-08.

[15] Keener, *Paul, Women & Wives*, 37.

both is God."[16] Keener concludes that nothing in this passage suggests the subordination of wives to their husbands.[17]

The fulcrum of controversy surrounds the phrase, "the man is the head of the woman," (1 Cor. 11:3). Therefore, it is imperative to examine The Foursquare Church position on this text. The Foursquare Church states that the phrase, "the man is the head of a woman" refers to the creation account of Eve; since the pre-incarnate Son took a rib from Adam and formed woman, Adam becomes the physical source of Eve.[18] The Foursquare Church further solidifies their position on women by affirming Paul's statement that women would be praying and prophesying publicly. This matter-of-fact statement lends no disapproval of the Apostle Paul.[19] Keener, in agreement with many other scholars, notes that to teach subordination from this passage, one would have to read subordination into the passage.[20]

Another challenging passage in the same letter is Paul's statement that "Women should be silent in the churches. For they are not permitted to speak but should be subordinate, as the law also says" (1 Cor. 14:34). Consideration must take into account whether Paul is giving an absolute truth like in the Ten Commandments (Exod. 20:2-17) or making a relative statement addressing a particular situation.[21] If Paul is saying that women should always keep silent, then he is contradicting himself because just three chapters earlier, he tells women to pray and prophesy (1 Cor. 11:5). Paul also instructs women on what to wear *when* they pray and prophesy in public (1 Cor. 11:4-5).

---

[16] Keener, *Paul, Women & Wives*, 38.

[17] Keener, *Paul, Women & Wives*, 47.

[18] Adams et al., *Women in Ministry Leadership*, 23.

[19] Adams et al., *Women in Ministry Leadership*, 25.

[20] Keener, *Paul, Women, & Wives*, 47.

[21] Gill and Caveness, *God's Women Then and Now*, 48.

J. M. Bassler more pointedly asks,

> How can women like Euodia and Syntyche (Phil 4:2-3),
> Prisca (Rom 16:3; 1 Cor 16:19), Mary (Rom 16:6), Junia
> (Rom 16:7), and Tryphaena and Tryphosa (Rom 16:12)
> function as co-workers in the church, if they cannot speak
> in those churches? How can Phoebe fulfil her role as deacon
> (Rom 16:1-2) if she cannot speak out in assembly? How can
> a woman like Nympha, who is influential enough to host a
> house church (Col 4:15), have been required to remain silent
> in her own home?[22]

Scripture points to numerous women publicly prophesying. Miriam
was a prophetess according to the Book of Exodus (Exod. 15:20-
21). After crossing the Red Sea, Miriam leads the women in praise
to God. Isaiah describes his wife as "the prophetess," exhibiting full
acceptance of her call (Isa. 8:3). Anna is the prophetess God used to
announce the arrival of the Messiah when baby Jesus was brought
to the temple (Luke 2:36-38). Philip had four daughters who were all
prophets (Acts 21:8-9). If Paul is commanding women to be silent
in the church, then it would contradict these examples of women,
whom God uses to declare his messages. If the statement by Paul (1
Cor. 14:34) was an absolute, then logically, women should be banned
from preaching, singing, praying, prophesying, exhorting, praising,
and encouraging.

Scripture points to numerous women publicly prophesying.

Scholars have interpreted 1 Corinthians 14:34 in numerous ways.
Craig Keener says this passage, "addresses disruptive questions in an

---

[22] Jouette M. Bassler, "1 Cor 12:3: Curse and Confession in
Context," *Journal of Biblical Literature* 101, no. 3 (1982): 415-418,
https://doi.org/10.2307/3260353.

environment where silence was expected of new learners (which most women were)."[23] Fee proposes that the setting was more like a Jewish synagogue with men on one side and women on the other and women were shouting out questions causing distractions in the service.[24] Of note, the term Paul uses to describe the behavior is "shameful" rather than disorderly. David Garland proposes that shame pertains to what society deems as inappropriate behavior in a given culture.[25] He describes the adjective "shameful" as being one where a wife defies convention by publicly embarrassing her husband by speaking in a public setting and thus questioning his authority concerning scrutiny of prophecy.[26]

In Christ, a person's spiritual potential is no longer limited.

Ben Witherington III claims that Paul's view on prophecy should be considered before tackling the text itself. He reminds readers that Paul not only encouraged women to prophesy but that prophecy, preaching, and teaching were functions that often overlapped, and nothing in 1 Corinthians 12-14 indicates that prophesying, teaching, or preaching was gender specific. Therefore, since 1 Corinthians 14:33-35 conflicts with other passages written by Paul, it appears to be a relative situational statement.

Another important Pauline passage to consider regarding women is "There is no longer Jew or Greek; there is no longer slave or free; there is no longer male and female, for all of you are one in Christ

---

[23] Craig S. Keener, "Interpretations and Applications of 1 Corinthians 14:34-35," Marg Mowczko, April 21, 2022, accessed July 12, 2022, https://margmowczko.com/interpretations-applications-1-cor-14_34-35.
[24] Fee, *The First Epistle to the Corinthians*, 703.
[25] David E. Garland, *1 Corinthians* (Grand Rapids, MI: Baker Academic, 2003), 664.
[26] Garland, *1 Corinthians*, 665.

Jesus. And if you belong to Christ, then you are Abraham's offspring, heirs according to the promise" (Gal. 3.28-29). In Christ, a person's spiritual potential is no longer limited. Everyone inherits the same promises. It is the believer's union with Christ that supersedes all other distinctions. Interesting parallels are notable when reading 1 Corinthians 12:13, "For in the one Spirit we were all baptized into one body—Jews or Greeks, slaves or free—and we were all made to drink of one Spirit," and in Colossians 3:11, "In that renewal there is no longer Greek and Jew, circumcised and uncircumcised, barbarian, Scythian, enslaved and free, but Christ is all and in all!" Witherington suggests that this repetition of pairs proposes that Paul is working with a pre-set piece in Galatians 3:28, meaning this text is a commentary on entrance requirements and the fact that neither social, sexual, nor ethnic differences affect whether one can be or remain in Christ.[27] Paul broke the pattern in Galatians to include the "male and female" phrase found in the creation account (Gen. 2), which also lies behind Paul's arguments in 1 Corinthians 11.[28] Perhaps Paul is making way for the single male or female in a culture where family relationships were anticipated.

In this passage, Paul declares to Timothy (who is assuming the pastorate of the Ephesian assembly) that a woman cannot teach or exercise authority over a man. However, this is the only biblical text explicating prohibiting women from teaching. Therefore, it is important to identify the cultural context of the passage prior to implementing the command as relevant beyond the current situation. Paul makes this statement in the church where Priscilla was a founding leader. This is also the church where Priscilla and her husband, Aquila, spent time discipling Apollos.

---

[27] Ben Witherington III, *Women and the Genesis of Christianity* (Cambridge: Cambridge University Press, 1999), 163.
[28] Witherington, *Women and the Genesis of Christianity*, 164.

In an example of Paul's affirmation of women, he writes, "I commend to you our sister Phoebe, a servant of the church at Cenchreae, that you may welcome her in the Lord in a way worthy of the saints, and help her in whatever she may need from you, for she has been a patron of many and of myself as well (Rom. 16:1-2). Was Paul contradicting himself to Timothy stating that women were disallowed to have authority over men in the church? The word for "authority" in this passage (1 Tim. 2:12) is *authentein*. It is not the more common term for authority, *exousia*. Paul uses *exousia* twelve times elsewhere in his letters. The word *authentein* is based on the personal pronoun for "self" meaning to exercise authority not given to them.[29] Based on this word study, Paul's purpose in this passage is to restrain anyone from placing themselves in a position over Timothy.

Interpretation of 1 Timothy 2:11-14 has caused tremendous suffering for women in all areas of profession. For example,

> A physician in family practice was summoned to her pastor's study and there was informed that her chosen medical specialty is outside God's will for her life. The pastor insisted that only two specialties are open to her: obstetrics/gynecology and pediatrics. The electrified young woman asked why God could not see fit to use her gifts in implementing healing for families. The answer was that 1 Timothy 2:12 forbade her having any authority over men, and that therefore she could not enter into a patient/physician relationship with a man. The woman left the church, went to a developing nation, and took up service as a missionary doctor, ministering in Jesus' name to all who came to her clinic.[30]

Paul teaches that all Scripture is inspired ("breathed out by God") and profitable for teaching (2 Tim. 3:16). Evidence of female leaders

---

[29] Adams et al., *Women in Ministry Leadership*, 40.
[30] Kroeger and Kroeger, *Suffer Not a Woman*, 11.

and teachers exists throughout Scripture. If God's purpose for women was for them to remain silent and avoid teaching and leading in the church, then proof of them doing so successfully would have been removed from the Scriptures, such as Junia and Priscilla. Furthermore, and the manifestation at Pentecost would have excluded women. As a result, 1 Timothy 2:11-15 appears to be a relative statement made by Paul to a unique situation within the Ephesian church.

Jesus's Response to, Respect for, and Release of Women

With the above examples of women leaders and a discussion of passages that create controversy, the project turns to Jesus and His view of women. To reiterate, God's purpose for equality for men and women is found in the creation account, continues in the stories of female leaders in the OT, and resonates with new authority in the life of Jesus. Not only did Jesus minister to women, but He also allowed women to minister to Him (Matt. 27:56, 61; Mark 15:40-41; Luke 8:1-3).

Jesus's ministry was inclusive.

Throughout the canonical Gospels, Jesus never mentions Eve's role in the entrance of sin. Instead, He allows women to follow him (which is not appropriate for a Rabbi), furthermore he is inclusive in his ministry to Jews and foreigners, to the sick and the well, the rich and the poor—no one is excluded (Mark 5:22-33; 7:24-30; 12:41-44; 15:40; Luke 10:25-37, 38-42; 8:2-3). Jesus's ministry was inclusive. The scriptural evidence lends confidence that God intended equality from the inception of creation, yet man has created hierarchy.

Jesus lived in a patriarchal society, yet He did not degrade women.[31] Jesus treated women as equal to men even though He broke social customs by allowing both men and women to follow Him. Young Jewish girls were not allowed to go to school, while young men could receive rabbinic mentoring and education. Women were required to stay in the women's court, one of the places where Jesus chose to teach.[32] This decision to include women reveals Jesus's desire for equity and exposes a difference between His view of women and that of other rabbis. Jesus also rejected the Jewish cultural principle that a woman's menstrual cycle caused her to be defiled or a source of defilement, excluding her from synagogue worship, feasts, and other cultic practices.[33] This action paved the way for women to travel with Jesus without restrictions (e.g., Luke 8:1-3). As Witherington notes, the relationship Jesus had with women led to the acceptance of women serving as valid witnesses and disciples of Jesus Christ.[34]

> Jesus lived in a patriarchal society, yet He did not degrade women.
> —Leonard Swidler

In the Gospel of Luke, Mary breaks cultural and social boundaries by sitting at the feet of Jesus, which is the posture of a male disciple (Luke 10:39), and Jesus responds to her behavior with these words: "Mary has chosen the better part, which will not be taken away from her" (Luke 10:42). N. T. Wright reminds us that a woman anointed Jesus, which is a priestly action, and Jesus allowed this to be done to

[31] Leonard Swidler, "Jesus Was a Feminist," God's Word to Women, January 1971, accessed July 15, 2022, https://www.godswordtowomen.org/feminist.htm.
[32] Gill and Cavaness, *God's Women Then and Now*, 73.
[33] Witherington, *Women and the Genesis of Christianity*, 86.
[34] Witherington, *Women and the Genesis of Christianity*, 120.

Him (John 11:2).[35] In Luke, Jesus is teaching on the Sabbath in a synagogue and notices a woman crippled for eighteen years (13:12-15). She was bent over and could not straighten herself. Jesus sees her, frees her from her disability, and the ruler of the synagogue rebukes Him for healing on the Sabbath. The religious leader's role is to care for his sheep, yet this ruler allows Mosaic Law to supersede the need of this woman; while Jesus responds in grace.[36] Jesus refers to this unnamed woman as a daughter of Abraham (Luke 13:16). Robert Stein posits that this rare title, "daughter of Abraham," indicates full inclusion of women giving her the authority to stand shoulder-to-shoulder with the sons of Abraham.[37]

In a patriarchal society, Jesus trusts, empowers, and sends women to proclaim His story.

The Samaritan woman in John 4 fulfills the role of disciple because she goes forth to share the good news of Jesus. Jews will not associate with Samaritans. However, Jesus transcends this gap of race and gender. This woman would have been considered unclean and unacceptable to Jesus's Jewish disciples. However, this account, directed toward non-Jews demonstrates how readers should respond to Christ—using this Samaritan woman—hated and despised by Jews—as an example.[38] She provides Jesus's real spiritual food to the

---

[35] "Prominent Biblical Scholars on Women in Ministry," Marg Mowczko, January 25, 2022, June 2, 2022, https://margmowczko.com/prominent-biblical-scholars-on-women-in-ministry.

[36] Williams, *How God Sees Women*, 315.

[37] Robert H. Stein, *The New American Commentary Series*, 42 vols., Logos Bible Software, 1992, accessed August 8, 2022, https://www.logos.com/product/55024/the-new-american-commentary-series, 374.

[38] Witherington, *Why Arguments Against Women in Ministry*, 233.

people while the Twelve can only share physical food from the village.

Jesus made some of the most significant revelations to women concerning Christianity.[39] He gave the first announcement of His messiahship to the woman at the well, who then became the first evangelist (John 4:7-42). He honored the poor widow by contributing two tiny coins while declaring her gift more than the others. Her gift was all she had, while others gave a portion of their wealth (Mark 12:43-44). Jesus commissioned women to testify on His behalf and to learn Hebrew Scripture (e.g., Mary) while rabbinic traditions forbade both.

> Jesus commissioned women to testify on
> His behalf and to learn Hebrew Scripture
> (e.g., Mary) while rabbinic traditions
> forbade both.

Throughout Scripture, Jesus never teaches the subordination of women. Deborah Gill and Barbara Cavaness describe His egalitarian style of teaching:

> Jesus balanced the parables with male and female activities so that both genders would receive the message. For example, He compared the kingdom of God to a mustard seed which a man planted and then to the years that a woman mixed in her dough (Luke 13:19-21). When teaching about lost sinners, Jesus used first a male shepherd who loses a sheep and then a woman who loses a coin as examples (Luke 15:3-10). He matched the parable of the persistent widow with the parable of the Pharisee and the tax collector to teach about justice (Luke 18:1-14). And He used both the story of the ten virgins and the story of the

---

[39] Gill and Cavaness, *God's Women Then and Now*, 75.

three servants to teach about the kingdom of heaven (Matt 25:1-30).[40]

Jesus heals, saves, restores, and includes women. In a patriarchal society, Jesus trusts, empowers, and sends women to proclaim His story.

Conclusion to Part One

In the creation account, Scripture defines male and female equality, excluding any suggestion of a hierarchal nature. In both Testaments examples of women leading are evident. However, a gap exists in the church when an androcentric interpretation of specific biblical passages that restrict women from leadership is accepted. As a result, complementarians believe that men and women are created equal yet should hold designated roles within the home and the church. At the same time, egalitarians judge that both men and women are equally created in God's image and gifted, placing no restrictions upon leadership roles within the church.[41]

In both Testaments examples of women leading are evident.

Therefore, Part One provides a biblical-theological foundation for examining the beliefs and practices of The Foursquare Church concerning female senior leadership. According to *Women in Ministry Leadership*, The Foursquare Church's goal is to ensure that every

---

[40] Gill and Cavaness, *God's Women Then and Now*, 75.
[41] Gretchen E. Ziegenhals, "Women in Ministry: Beyond the Impasse," Baylor University Center for Christian Ethics, 2009, accessed July 13, 2022,
https://www.baylor.edu/content/services/document.php/98766.pdf.

woman called and gifted by God has open access to mentoring, equipping, and opportunities to lead.[42] This statement endorses what Part One has emphasized, that the Word of God includes women as equal partners in ministry with men. If accurate, then the study should reveal that The Foursquare Church facilitates women to achieve their highest calling, including leadership.

---

[42] Adams et al., *Women in Ministry Leadership*, 6.

PART TWO

The Foursquare Church has affirmed women in ministry leadership since its inception. The following positional statement gives further confidence that the institution supports the expectation and anticipation of women actively leading in every role within the church.

> The Great Commission, along with the need of the dying world in which we live, calls for all the people of God, His sons and daughters, to engage the harvest using whatever gifts he has entrusted to them. Since women are redeemed, anointed, gifted, called and loved by God in exactly the same way as men, we categorically affirm that they should be fully released to exercise their gifts for every facet of ministry in His church. Anyone called by God and verified through character, spiritual experience and preparation for service or leadership, is qualified for Foursquare Church ministry in any role or office, regardless of gender, age, or ethnicity.[1]

Nevertheless, the question of why there is underrepresentation of female senior leaders within The Foursquare Church remains. To evaluate this concern, Part Two includes current statistics, barriers, and studies on the experiences of women seeking or in leadership roles.

---

[1] Jim Adams, "Position Statements," in *Women in Ministry Leadership: A Summary of the Biblical Position of the Foursquare Church Concerning God's Grace and a Woman's Potential under His Sovereignty and Call*, rev. ed., ed. Steve Schell (Los Angeles: Foursquare Media, 2021), 9.

Although many women today enter careers previously inaccessible, specific occupations retain a disparity in leadership based on gender.[2] Repeating behaviors in a male-dominated culture promote male authority and female submission.[3] Beth Barr notes that evangelical teachings that subordinate women in the home and the church also influence attitudes about women in the workplace.[4] Patriarchy, whether Christian or pagan, is still a patriarchy,[5] and "[b]oth systems place power in the hands of men and take power away from women teaching that women rank lower than men. ... [and] that their voices are worth less than the voices of men."[6] Just as Junia, Huldah, and Phoebe experienced the challenge of living in a patriarchal society, women today face a similar challenge.[7]

Patriarchy, whether Christian or pagan, is still a patriarchy.
—Beth Allison Barr

Although a woman, Aimee Semple McPherson, founded The Foursquare Church, since her death there have only been male presidents and male-dominated executive leadership positions.[8] A

---

[2] T. H. Alaqahtani, "The Status of Women in Leadership," Research Gate, accessed July 6, 2022, https://www.researchgate.net/profile/Tahani-Alqahtani-2/publication/340514638_The_Status_of_Women_in_Leadership/links/60580b44458515e8345ff7bd/The-Status-of-Women-in-Leadership.pdf, 294-299.

[3] Beth Allison Barr, *The Making of Biblical Womanhood: How the Subjugation of Women Became Gospel Truth* (Grand Rapids: Brazos Press, 2021),14.

[4] Barr, *The Making of Biblical Womanhood*, 18.

[5] Barr, *The Making of Biblical Womanhood*, 18.

[6] Barr, *The Making of Biblical Womanhood*, 18.

[7] Scot McKnight, *The Blue Parakeet: Rethinking How You Read the Bible*, 2nd ed. (Grand Rapids, MI: Zondervan, 2018), 297.

[8] See "History," The Foursquare Church, May 30, 2022, accessed August 2, 2022, https://www.foursquare.org/about/history for a list of the presidents: "Aimee Semple McPherson (1923-1944), Rolf K. McPherson (1944-1988), John Holland (1988-1997), Harold Helms (1997-1998,

woman was not simply *present* at the birth of The Foursquare movement; she was the *deliverer*—the founder and president of the movement. She was not just the voice of *a* woman but the voice for *all* women.

A woman was not simply *present* at the
birth of The Foursquare movement;
she was the *deliverer*—the founder
and president of the movement.
She was not just the voice
of *a* woman but the voice
for *all* women.

---

interim), Paul Risser (1998-2004), Jared Roth (2004, interim), Jack Hayford (2004-2009), Glenn Burris, Jr. (2009-2020), and Randy Remington (2020-present)."

Chapter 4

What *Was*: Looking Back at Foursquare

Foursquare's Founding Timeline

The Foursquare Church, founded in 1910, rests upon a biblical foundation and looks to the Old and New Testaments for exemplars in ministry. As prophets, women in the Old Testament led and spoke on God's behalf (Miriam: Exod. 15:20; Deborah: Judg. 4:4 Huldah: 2 Kings 22:14; 2 Chron. 34:22; and Noadiah: Neh. 6:14). In the New Testament, they functioned as prophets and disciples holding various leadership roles (Anna: Luke 2:36; Phoebe: Rom. 16:1-2; Junias: Rom. 16:7; Philip's daughters: Acts 21:9). Although the Church has been slow to embrace the New Testament idea of mutuality and equality, God has chosen, anointed, and appointed male and female leaders. Hebrews 13:8 remains foundational to The Foursquare Church and can be found in sanctuaries worldwide: "Jesus Christ is the same yesterday and today and forever." This Scripture serves as hope for women within its institution who trust that what God did in its founder, He will continue to do in its daughters.

The Foursquare Church's timeline details the following seven events that Sister McPherson establishes—many unprecedented feats by a woman.

- In 1910, Sister McPherson returns home from a mission trip to China as a single twenty-year-old mom and widow.

51

- In 1918, McPherson starts cross-country evangelism by automobile and boldly began asking God for healing to take place in her gatherings, which were later confirmed by medical reports.

- In 1923, she becomes the pastor of Angeles Temple, previously called, "Echo Park Revival Tabernacle," in Los Angeles, which will eventually host services in five languages.

- In the same year, she founds the First Foursquare Bible institute (known today as Life Pacific University) to train and send out men and women as ministers; and the first church plant occurs.

- By February 1924, McPherson becomes the first woman to own a major radio station and uses it to preach the gospel and sends the first missionaries to India. After establishing one hundred churches, steps are taken to incorporate the International Church of the Foursquare Gospel (ICFG).

- On December 28, 1927, the International Church of the Foursquare Gospel becomes incorporated.

- In August 1928, McPherson establishes the first commissary to feed, clothe more than 1.5 million people during the Great Depression while providing medical supplies for the local immigrants and poor Los Angelinos.[1]

---

[1] "History," The Foursquare Church, May 30, 2022, accessed August 2, 2022, https://www.foursquare.org/about/history. Regarding the commissary, an Associated Press writer reports, "In the last eleven months the 'commissary' of the temple provided free groceries to 40,110 persons or 10,769 families." See "Angelus Temple Gives Aid to Thousands of Needy: Free Dining Has Also Been Opened," *The Florence Times*, March 18, 1932, 2. The support and care of those in need in Los Angeles provided by McPherson's commissary gave her city and national recognition as a community leader (Ibid.).

In addition, her contribution to Los Angeles was a visual reminder of her political power within the city.[2]

Today, The Foursquare Church, consists of 8.8 million members, with one of the critical pillars of the denomination being service.[3] Nevertheless, the good works McPherson accomplished did not avert the gender discrimination she experienced in her ministry, as she notes,

> Someone came up to me and said, "I don't like to hear a woman preach." Well, I don't blame you—really I don't. I don't like to hear a woman preach either. And I don't like to hear a man preach. I like to hear the Holy Ghost preach. God grant that we will get to the place where we see neither male nor female, but Jesus Christ exalted and lifted up, and the messenger hidden behind the Cross [sic].[4]

Aimee's love for truth, the conviction of the assignment, her reliance on Holy Spirit, and the urgency of sharing the gospel overrode the challenges concerning gender.

Aimee's love for truth, the conviction of the assignment, her reliance on Holy Spirit, and the urgency of sharing the gospel overrode the challenges concerning gender.

While teaching a class at L.I.F.E. Bible College, McPherson said of Foursquare's advocacy of women in ministry,

---

[2] Leah Payne, *Gender and Pentecostal Revivalism: Making a Female Ministry in the Early Twentieth Century* (New York: Palgrave MacMillan, 2015), 93.
[3] "Beliefs," Foursquare, accessed August 2, 2022, https://www.Foursquare.org/about/beliefs/.
[4] Aimee Semple McPherson, *Real Aimee* (Los Angeles, CA: Foursquare Media, 2022), 34.

This is the only church, I am told, that is ordaining women preachers. This [a major Pentecostal denomination] are not [any longer] ordaining women, to my knowledge … Foursquaredom is the only work that has given such acknowledgment to women preachers, as well as men. Even the Pentecostal works in some cases, have said, "No women preachers." But I am opening the door, and as long as Sister McPherson is alive, she is going to hold the door open and say, "Ladies come!"[5]

Additionally, as a denomination founded in diversity, The Foursquare Church has advocated multicultural leadership from its beginning. As Jim Adams asserts, "foursquare" means to "take a bold stand firm, forthright, unwavering in conviction," and The Foursquare Church is founded on this bold and biblical brassiness concerning God's truth and speaking this truth in love (Eph 4:15).[6] With this same boldness, The Foursquare Church anchors its support for women in ministry leadership.

Who We Are

In the early 1970s, Foursquare President Rolph McPherson, son of Aimee Semple McPherson, replied to members of the Pentecostal Fellowship of North America by stating, "If we are Pentecostal, we need to say we believe in initial evidence"; "after a few moments of reflection [he] replied, genuinely, 'But we're not Pentecostal; we're Foursquare.'"[7] The Foursquare Church is a Pentecostal organization

---

[5] Jack W. Hayford, *Women in Leadership Ministry*, ed. Steve Schell (Los Angeles: Foursquare Media, 2007), 66.

[6] Adams et al., *Women in Ministry Leadership*, 13.

[7] This account was relayed by Dr. Paul Risser, former Foursquare President (1998-2004) via Steve Overman. Overman serves The Foursquare Church on the Doctrine Committee, the Education Commission, the Missions and National Church Committees, the Board of Directors, and as Supervisor of the Willamette District from 2002-2009. He serves as a member of the Board of Regents at George Fox Evangelical Seminary in Portland, Oregon. Quoted by Rick Mathis,

with roots and spiritual experiences of its founder tracing back to the early Pentecostal revivals held at Azusa Street. Rolph McPherson's statement correctly assumes that there is more to defining The Foursquare Church than simply referring to it as Pentecostal. Jack Hayford makes a helpful dissimilarity between Pentecostal with an uppercase 'P' and pentecostal with a lowercase 'p.' "He asserts that Pentecostals are primarily concerned with the doctrine of initial evidence … while pentecostals practice prophetic speech (glossolalia) regularly with missional effect."[8] According to Aaron Friesen, Hayford's definition better articulates the essential Pentecostal experience for Foursquare.[9]

The Foursquare Church released a project in 2018 called The Foursquare Identity Keystones, including five identifiers.[10] Sam Rockwell writes that in establishing these Identity Keystones, The Foursquare Church defined its "domain of expertise" while differentiating itself among its peer institutions.[11] These identity markers expose what is central, distinctive, and enduring about the organization.[12] "Foursquare Identity Stones" emerged from the

---

"Disciple-Making in Foursquare Missioning," *QUADRUM: Journal of the Foursquare Scholars Fellowship*, no. 2 (November 2018), 197.

[8] Jack Hayford, "The Pentecostal Pilgrimage and the Emerging Church," Second Annual Pentecostal Leaders Series, The Wilson Institute for Pentecostal Studies," Costa Mesa, CA, February 17, 2011, quoted by Gary Tyra, *The Holy Spirit in Mission: Prophetic Speech and Action in Christian Witness* (Downers Grove, IL: IVP Academic, 2011), 60.

[9] Aaron Friesen, *Foursquare Identity Keystones* (Los Angeles, CA: Foursquare Media, 2018), 7.

[10] Sam Rockwell, "Denominational Identity and Ministerial Identity Congruence within the Foursquare Church" (PhD diss., Fielding Graduate University, Santa Barbara, CA, 2013), ProQuest, accessed August 1, 2022, https://www.proquest.com/dissertations-theses/denoninational-identity-ministerial-congruence/docview/1316620367/se-2.

[11] Sam Rockwell, ed., *Identity Keystones: What Makes Us Foursquare* (Los Angeles, CA: The Foursquare Church, 2017), 25.

[12] Rockwell, *Identity Keystones*, 18.

history and practices of The Foursquare Church in tandem with current work concerning its identity, as noted in Table 1 below.[13]

Table 1. Foursquare Identity Stones[14]

Foursquare Keystones	Identity Markers
Five Significant Areas of Identity Congruence	What makes us Foursquare
1. Pentecostal Ethos	Exhibiting
2. Moderation	Exhibiting
3. Women in Senior Leadership	Advancing
4. Integrated Mission	Upholding
5. Indigenous Empowerment	Practicing

Pentecostal Ethos

The Foursquare Church lists Pentecostal Ethos as the expectancy of Spirit baptism and spiritual gifts, speaking in tongues, physical healing, passionate and expressive worship, and present-day miracles in its culture.[15] It represents the ways of living out and embracing the work and power of the Holy Spirit.

Moderation

Moderation, the second keystone, is considered "central to the whole idea of a Foursquare movement"[16] and continues as a guiding value for its leadership. These values are expressed in moderate public worship, mediating doctrinal positions, interdenominational spirit, and cultural discernment.[17] This "middle-of-the-road" stance is described as, "in the essentials unity, in the non-essentials liberty,

---

[13] Rockwell, *Identity Keystones.*
[14] Friesen, ed. *Foursquare Identity Keystones*, 5.
[15] Friesen, ed. *Foursquare Identity Keystones*, 11.
[16] Friesen, *Foursquare Identity Keystones*, 11.
[17] Friesen, *Foursquare Identity Keystones*, 11.

and in all things charity."[18] The Foursquare Church includes a statement on moderation in its Declaration of Faith.

> We believe that (Phil 4:5) the moderation of the believer should be known to all men; that his experience and daily walk should never lead him (Eph 4:14, 15) into extremes, fanaticism, (1 Cor 13:5) unseemly manifestations, back-bitings [sic], murmurings; but that his sober, thoughtful, balanced, (Col 3:12, 13) mellow, forgiving, and zealous Christian experience should be one of steadfast uprightness, equilibrium, humility, self-sacrifice and Christlikeness.[19]

McPherson defined the manifestation of the Holy Spirit differently.[20] Her stand on moderation appears throughout the history of The Foursquare Church.

Women in Senior Leadership

Women in Senior Leadership is the third marker. At a baccalaureate sermon preached in 1930, Aimee Semple McPherson said,

> There are some who believe that a woman should never witness for Jesus Christ—that her lips should be sealed. This is not according to the Word of God ... I would bring a message to my sisters just now: "Go on with the Word of God!" God has used the womenfolks! [sic] ...Through the

---

[18] "This is Foursquare: Cabinet Report 2022," Foursquare Leader, accessed August 3, 2022, https://foursquare-leader.s3.us-east-1.amazonaws.com/about_us/business/2022-Cabinet-Report.pdf, 12.
[19] Aimee Semple McPherson, "International Church of the Foursquare Gospel," Declaration of Faith, accessed August 1, 2022, https://foursquare-leader.s3.us-east-1.amazonaws.com/about_us/business/Bylaws_English_2019.pdf.
[20] McPherson asserts that to be Pentecostal in Spirit means something far different than what many suppose. She made this statement in response to a complaint by Assemblies of God leaders present during a revival gathering. The leaders questioned in their official publication whether McPherson was truly Pentecostal, as she requested that the expressions of the Spirit be held until a more fitting time.

centuries I seem to see them coming; these witnesses, these precious women of God … an unbroken, steady line of heroic womanhood! It was not only yesterday that the Lord used women, He has used them since time began and is still using them.[21]

As in the above communication, McPherson often clarified her position while addressing women in ministry through speech or writing. She emphasized preaching the gospel, proclaiming healing, Holy Spirit empowerment, and the imminent return of Christ, representing the four squares of the Church's logo.[22] McPherson honored and encouraged both males and females in leadership ministry believing women should have absolute equality with men in preaching, serving in all leadership roles, and fulfilling the Great Commission.[23] Although much of the founder's story and ministry provide a tangible witness contributing to The Foursquare Church's position in support of women, evidence exists that Aimee Semple McPherson felt challenged by the influence of the turn-of-the-century view, in which the primary role of a woman is as a mother and wife (i.e., in subordination to her husband).[24] McPherson licensed and ordained women in great numbers; however, she "only occasionally placed women in top leadership position[s] … [and] when women had children the man assumed the role as pastor."[25]

[21] Aimee Semple McPherson, "The Servants and the Handmaidens," *The Bridal Call Foursquare* 13, no. 9 (February 1930): 5.
[22] "Beliefs," Foursquare, accessed August 2, 2022, https://www.Foursquare.org/about/beliefs/. This what foursquare means. The logo of the church is the symbolic representation of the four standards.
[23] Adams et al., *Women in Ministry Leadership*, 52.
[24] Janet Hassey, *No Time for Silence* (Grand Rapids, MI: Zondervan, 1986), 7.
[25] Nathaniel Van Cleave, *The Vine and the Branches: A History of the International Church of the Foursquare Gospel* (Los Angeles: International Church of the Foursquare Gospel, 1992), 42.

McPherson was not only concerned with
the "one" soul; she was passionate about
the salvation as well as the physical
welfare of her city.

Perhaps these early positional inconsistencies by The Foursquare Church founder explain the significant gap between male and female leadership representation especially at the senior pastor level and higher.

Integrated Mission

The fourth keystone is Integrated Mission. This represents the passion of the denomination's founder for evangelism and community provision. McPherson was not only concerned with the "one" soul; she was passionate about the salvation as well as the physical welfare of her city. Her response to meeting people's physical needs included feeding the hungry, clothing those in need, comforting the lonely, and helping the sick.[26]

Indigenous Empowerment

Finally, the fifth marker of Foursquare identity, Indigenous Empowerment, involves the practice of finding and preparing leaders to lead in their context: ethnically, culturally, geographically, and locally.[27] From Foursquare's origin, missions has been at the core of its identity. In a 1927 *Bridal Call* article, McPherson writes,

> Angeles Temple is opening one of the mightiest missionary enterprises that has ever been started. Nothing short of establishing missionaries and mission stations in every land and among ever kindred, tribe and tongue will satisfy these

---

[26] Friesen, *Foursquare Identity Keystones*, 25.
[27] "Friesen, *Foursquare Identity Keystones*, 29.

earnest, enthusiastic and consecrated followers of the Foursquare Gospel, "The field is the world" is their motto, and "Around the world with the Foursquare Gospel" is their slogan. The spirit of the Foursquare Gospel is that of the true pioneer.[28]

Her passion for souls traveled far beyond Los Angeles. She was committed to worldwide evangelism before she founded The Foursquare Church. The Book of Acts influenced McPherson with the inclusion of all people.[29] Hence, her desire to multiply, spread, and train allowed the teaching of the gospel in all languages. Foursquare Missions International (FMI) currently operates in 156 nations and territories, partnering with 100,000 churches, and growing.[30] The Foursquare Church remains committed to mobilizing leaders with training and resourcing to spread the good news around the globe.

She was committed to worldwide evangelism before she founded The Foursquare Church.

The Foursquare 2022 Cabinet Report provides evidence of several keystones within The Foursquare Church—omitting "Moderation" and "Integrated Mission," since these are both impossible to record.

---

[28] Aimee Semple McPherson, "Foursquare Gospel World-Wide Missions," *Foursquare Bridal Call* 11 (October 1927): 15.

[29] McPherson, "Foursquare Gospel World-Wide Missions," 15.

[30] "Foursquare Missions International," Foursquare Missions International, accessed May 25, 2022, https://www.foursquaremissions.org/.

Table 2. Foursquare Cabinet Report[31]

2021 Foursquare by the Numbers	Current Information
Pentecostal Ethos	Salvation: 134,439 Holy Spirit Baptism: 6,472 Baptisms by water: 7,445 Healing: 21,362
Moderation	No evidence reported
Women in Senior Leadership	Females licensed: 2675 (39.1%) Senior Female leaders: 132 (9%)
Integrated Mission	No evidence reported
Indigenous Empowerment	68,500 churches in 150 countries, with 1700 in the U.S.

The statistics in Table 2 concerning women within the denomination warrants further explanation. The report shows total ministers in Foursquare as 6,844 (4,169 males and 2,675 female). Within this 60.9 percent male representation and 39.1 percent female representation, only 9.4 percent of churches within its denomination are currently led by women. The report confirms 1,279 male senior pastors and 132 female senior pastors.

The Foursquare Church executes its corporate business through a president, board of directors, the cabinet and, an executive council.[32] However, the highest seat of authority is the convention body,[33]

---

[31] "This is Foursquare: Cabinet Report 2022," 3.
[32] "Introducing the Foursquare Church," The Foursquare Church, accessed July 9, 2022, http://foursquare-org.s3.amazonaws.com/resources/Print_Brochure_Introducing_Foursquare_Church_English_bw.pdf.
[33] According to the 2019 Foursquare Church Bylaws 5.5.c, the convention body constitutes delegates from Foursquare churches: one delegate for each fifty members or fraction thereof from each Foursqare church located in the United States of America. International Church of The Foursquare Gospel, "Corporate Bylaws 2019 Edition," Foursquare

which alone has the authority to make or amend the bylaws of the Church.[34] The Executive Board of Directors, defined in the bylaws as the official body of The Foursquare Church, oversees the carrying out of the objects and purposes directly stated in the Articles and Bylaws.[35]

The directors are collectively referred to as the Board and consist of not less than twelve and not more than twenty-five members.[36] Currently, the board comprises twenty-four members, with five of those roles held by women. The denomination divides its districts into six segments—Northwest, Pacific, Western, Atlantic, Central, and National Hispanic—serving all the United States. District supervisors devote themselves to the strengthening and multiplication of Foursquare churches within their respective districts per the Articles and Bylaws. The Foursquare Church currently has one of the six supervisory appointments held by a woman, with six female associate supervisors. With the district supervisor aware of opportunities and the power to appoint credentialed women to available positions, this is a significant role, yet only one female currently holds this position in the United States.

In the 2022 Foursquare Church Cabinet Report, Points of Action were reported, including setting expectations for welcoming women to lead, preach, and be in the room.[37] Their desire is to create a standard where pulpit culture embraces women as the norm.[38] The intentionality to create a point of action incorporating women in the pulpit as the norm, I suggest, discloses the denomination's inability to do so successfully to date.

Leader, accessed July 4, 2022, https://foursquare-leader.s3.us-east-1.amazonaws.com/about_us/business/Bylaws_English.pdf.

[34] "Introducing the Foursquare Church."

[35] Foursquare, "Corporate Bylaws 2019 Edition."

[36] Foursquare, "Corporate Bylaws 2019 Edition."

[37] "This is Foursquare: Cabinet Report 2022," 11.

[38] "This is Foursquare: Cabinet Report 2022," 11.

On February 6, 1923, Aimee Semple McPherson responded to a call from God to "Gather together those who have consecrated their lives to the service and give them the benefit of your fourteen years of practical training. Then send them out to answer these calls."[39] The purpose of a Bible institute was to practically train and equip students to preach the Foursquare gospel. The institution began one month after the opening of Angeles Temple.[40] Within two years, *The Bridal Call* states that the Institute's students had birthed twenty-nine churches. The Institute began with fifty students, and by its fifth year, the student body numbered 800.[41]

August 1, 2019, serves as a monumental day within The Foursquare Church with the first woman to take the helm of Life Pacific University since its 1920s founder, Aimee Semple McPherson. On that day, Dr. Angie Richey became the eleventh president of The Foursquare Church's affiliate institution. At the time of her installation, the university reported close to 700 students, residential and online. She commented on the humbling experience of following in the footsteps of Foursquare's great founder and continuing Sister's vision for the university.[42]

The enrollment at Life Pacific University in the 2020-2021 academic year is 551 students with 250 male and 351 female.[43] With 41.6 percent Hispanic/Latino, 37.9 percent white, and 5.1 percent black/African American, the makeup of the university appears to

---

[39] "Foursquare Ministry Training," Foursquare Leader, accessed April 1, 2022, https://foursquare-leader.s3.amazonaws.com/education/Institutes_Handbook.pdf.

[40] "Foursquare Ministry Training."

[41] "Foursquare Ministry Training."

[42] Andy Butcher, "Life Pacific University Appoints Angie Richey as President," News + Resources (The Foursquare Church, August 1, 2019), https://resources.foursquare.org/life-pacific-university-appoints-angie-richey-as-president/.

[43] "Institutional Data and Disclosures," Life Pacific University, January 1, 2022, https://lifepacific.edu/about/institutional-data-and-disclosures/.

represent its founder's vision, as over 60 percent of the LPU student body is made up of historically under-represented populations. Additionally, the report states that the licensing panel approved 100 percent of students pursuing Foursquare licensing, and 63 percent of those students had an immediate place of ministry.

The Foursquare Church reports that from its humble beginnings as a two-year single location college, Life Pacific University is now a four-year educational institution."[44] Since its founding, approximately 27,000 students have completed some form of study at the denomination's flagship institution.[45] In addition, The Foursquare Church continues to include and support women in training and preparation for the call to ministry through academic support.

The Foursquare Church published a handbook for women in ministry leadership, clarifying the denomination's commitment to valuing every woman, equipping her, and giving her an opportunity.[46] It includes their positional statements, the biblical basis for women in ministry, the history of Foursquare leaders, and proposed actions for continued progress.[47] To further mobilize female leaders (as well as men) with a deeper theological foundation, toward that end, in early 2022, a three-part video series was prepared which includes (1) a comprehensive review from the Old and New Testament studying women in ministry leadership providing a solid and healthy hermeneutic; (2) an unpacking of Paul's prohibitions delving into specific questions such as, "Why did Paul write these words? What should the church do with these words?"; and (3) an offer of hope to women and to the church at large. The hope is that

---

[44] "History and Heritage," Life Pacific College, accessed January 5, 2023, https://lifepacific.edu/about/history-heritage/.
[45] Butcher, "Life Pacific University Appoints Angie Richey as President."
[46] Adams et al., *Women in Ministry Leadership*, 6.
[47] Adams et al., *Women in Ministry Leadership*, 6.

once the church fully understands the topic concerning women that the focus can once again be on the harvest.[48]

These factors reveal The Foursquare Church's support of women aggressively moves forward with intentionality. Multiple opportunities are available to equip, mentor, and connect female ministry leaders to other female leaders within the denomination. The Foursquare Church reports several leadership cohort opportunities hosted by various Foursquare leaders across the country. These include the following:

> ## The Foursquare Church continues to fall short, with female leaders dramatically underrepresented in all areas of service.

---

(1) Women in Ministry Leadership, which seeks to catapult female leaders into new levels of Spirit-empowered leadership. This cohort is an annual, seven-month intensive offered to female ministry leaders seeking mentoring, coaching, community, equipping, and empowerment. This cohort includes assessments and leadership resources, collaborative and cohort-style learning, an expanded leadership network, prayer and prophetic ministry, and a summit gathering.

(2) Immersion Leadership, which provides an opportunity for women to connect with other female leaders, gain wisdom and engage in God's unique purpose for their lives. This opportunity is provided through an eight-month cohort experience of topical

---

[48] "Video: 'Women in Leadership Ministry' Series with Jerry Dirmann," News + Resources, January 30, 2020, accessed August 31, 2022, https://resources.foursquare.org/video/video-women-in-leadership-ministry-series-with-jerry-dirmann/. This video series was created for individuals being licensed, so they would understand the stance of The Foursquare Church on women in ministry leadership.

teaching, life-coaching, mentoring, spiritual gift assessments, counseling, and developing relationships with a wide variety of women leaders.

(3) Cultivate for Women Leaders, a seven-month cohort experience where participants develop core leadership competencies and strengthen their call of ministry. The purpose of Cultivate is to coach and connect women leaders within a relational learning environment.

(4) Women in Ministry Leadership, Oregon Cohort, which coaches and connects with key female leaders in a relational learning environment for multiplication of women leaders, development of core competencies, future sponsoring, and to create a cultural commitment to the holistic development of women in ministry leadership.[49]

Each of these cohorts is available to women who sense a call to leadership within The Foursquare Church.

Although a remarkable effort to support women through various resources, the underrepresentation of women in all areas of leadership remains a concern. The Foursquare Church continues to fall short, with female leaders dramatically underrepresented in all areas of service. Karen Tremper agrees with this assessment: "Despite a consistent theological stance in support of the equality of men and women at all levels of church leadership, Foursquare has faced various struggles and challenges putting this belief into practice at an organizational and local congregational level."[50] Statistics within The Foursquare Church substantiate a significant gap

---

[49] "Women in Ministry Leadership Resources," News + Resources, February 5, 2022, https://resources.foursquare.org/link/women-in-ministry-leadership-resources/.

[50] Karen Tremper, "Advancing Women in Senior Leadership," in *Identity Keystones: What Makes Us Foursquare*, ed. Sam Rockwell (Los Angeles, CA: The Foursquare Church, 2017), 58-81.

between male and female leadership particularly at the senior pastor level and higher.[51] The gap between male and female representation encourages further inquiry regarding women holding senior leadership roles in other denominations compared to those within The Foursquare Church.

Conclusion

The desire of the founder of The Foursquare Church was to include women in ministry leadership. Evidence of female leaders—planting, leading, and serving—appears throughout the history of the denomination. Expectations for female leadership is incorporated in the defining keystones of the institution, and a positional statement exists affirming women at all levels of leadership, and there is evidence of ongoing efforts to train and equip women for leadership opportunities.

---

[51] Tremper, "Advancing Women in Senior Leadership," 70.

Chapter 5

What *Is*: Women in Ministry Leadership Today

Introduction

In light of what has been within The Foursquare Church, this section briefly examines the nature of female leadership in the political, corporate, academic, and church sectors as a way of considering the present situation in order to lay the groundwork for what can be—and needs to be—in the future.

Female Leadership in Political, Corporate, and Academic Sectors

In 2017, Barna Group investigated "What Americans Think about Women in Power."[1] Barna reports that in the corporate sector, women enjoy overall support among the general population with, 94 percent of Americans comfortable with a female CEO.[2] According to Fortune 500, the number of women in corporate leadership has reached an all-time high, with forty-one CEOs spearheading

---

[1] David Kinnaman, "What Americans Think about Women in Power," Barna Group, March 8, 2017, accessed August 3, 2022, https://www.barna.com/research/americans-think-women-power.
[2] Kinnaman, "What Americans Think about Women in Power."

America's largest companies.[3] The company reports that female CEOs are finding staying power and stability at the top.[4]

Regarding the political sector, Barna's research identifies that 85 percent of Americans feel comfortable with the possibility of a female in the White House (85 percent men and 86 percent women, with 98 percent Democrats and 65 percent Republicans).[5] Although Americans affirm the possibility of a female president, Article II of the Constitution sends mixed signals: "The executive Power shall be vested in a President of the United States of America. He shall hold his Office during the Term of four Years, and, together with the Vice-President chosen for the same Term, be elected, as follows."[6]

Although Americans affirm the possibility of a female president, Article II of the Constitution sends mixed signals: "The executive Power shall be vested in a President of the United States of America. He shall …

With the pronouns "he" and "his," it appears that the Constitution assumes the role of the President as male.[7] Currently, a female, the first in history, holds the position of Vice-President, and in case of

---

[3] Emma Hinchliffe, "Roz Brewer, Thasunda Brown Duckett, Karen Lynch Make up Record Number of Female Fortune 500 CEOS," Fortune, May 23, 2022, accessed August 3, 2022, https://fortune.com/2022/05/23/female-ceos-fortune-500-2022-women-record-high-karen-lynch-sarah-nash.
[4] Emma Hinchliffe, "Roz Brewer."
[5] Kinnaman, "What Americans Think about Women in Power."
[6] "Executive Power: An Overview," Legal Information Institute, accessed July 22, 2022, https://www.law.cornell.edu/wex/executive_power.
[7] Philip B. Payne and Vince Huffaker, *Why Can't Women Do That?: Breaking Down the Reasons Churches Put Men in Charge* (Boulder, CO: Vinati Press,2021), 47.

an emergency, she would fill the role of President of the United States. In addition, twelve female cabinet and cabinet-level positions are held by women, four women currently serve on the United States Supreme Court, and 147 or 27.5 percent of seats in Congress (twenty-four in the U.S. Senate and 123 in the U.S. House) are held by women.[8] However, an analysis conducted by Diana Tal and Avishag Gordon shows support for women in politics diminishes in married couples, older Americans, those who consider themselves religious.[9]

> Forty-three percent of the top 200
> universities have a female leader.
> — Times Higher Education World University Rankings

Regarding university leadership, the Times Higher Education World University Rankings describe that "Forty-three percent of the top 200 universities have a female leader."[10] The report names the University of Oxford as the number one institution in higher education; Oxford and three Ivy League Universities—the University of Pennsylvania, Cornell University, and Brown University—all have female presidents.[11]

---

[8] "Current Numbers," Center for American Women and Politics, accessed July 4, 2022, https://cawp.rutgers.edu/facts/current-numbers.

[9] Diana Tal and Avishag Gordon, "Women as Political Leaders: A Bibliometric Analysis of the Literature." *Society* 55, no 3 (June 2018): 256-61, https://www.proquest.com/scholarly-journals/women-as-political-leaders-bibliometric-analysis/docview/2036586925/se-2?accountid=40702.

[10] Times Higher Education, "World University Rankings," Times Higher Education (THE), accessed June 8, 2022, https://www.timeshighereducation.com/world-university-rankings/2022/world-ranking#!/page/0/length/25/sort_by/rank/sort_order/asc/cols/stats.

[11] Times Higher Education, "World University Rankings."

The evidence of female leaders in academia, politics, and corporations validates representation of female leaders at some of the highest levels of authority throughout the country. However, female leaders in the church remains lower than in the secular system.

Female Senior Leadership within the Church

Women play a significant role in the spread of Christianity. The foundation of revival during the Second Great Awakening and the Azusa Street revival resulted from a network of female organizers who made it their goal to convert their husbands and children.[12] To a degree, one could consider Christianity as a women's movement since two-thirds of its active participants are female.[13] Women have made a pivotal impact upon advancing God's Kingdom for hundreds of years, yet they still struggle with discrimination within the Church.

Women play a significant role in the spread of Christianity.

Despite the discouragement of lingering controversial religious doctrine, women persistently contend for positions in the church in obedience to their sense of God's call, as did Aimee Semple McPherson. In 1853, Antoinette Brown became the first woman ordained to pastoral ministry in the United States.[14] Eventually,

---

[12] Dana L. Robert, "World Christianity as a Women's Movement," *International Bulletin of Mission Research* 30, issue 4 (January 1, 2006), 183, https://doi.org/10.1177/239693930603000403.

[13] Robert, "World Christianity," 180.

[14] Jessica York, "Antoinette Brown and Olympia Brown," Signs of Our Faith Series, 2013, Unitarian Universalist Association, July 21, 2017, accessed August 10, 2022,

Brown resigned from her position, yet undaunted joined the Unitarians in 1863 and was again ordained.[15] In a 2018 survey by Kimberly Ervin Alexander and James Bowers of female leaders within the Church of God regarding the disparity in women in authority roles, the unanimous response of the participants is, "They have a sure call from God and will not be stopped!"[16] As Joseph demonstrated to Potiphar, to shut him out was to shut out the source of blessing,[17] and as the writer of Hebrews states, "of whom the world was not worthy" (Heb. 11:38-39). One cannot help but ask whether the work to silence and erase God's purpose for women in the church could mean condemning those to hell who would not hear the gospel otherwise.

Churches are filled with over 50 percent of women in their congregations yet they remain significantly underrepresented in senior-level leadership roles.[18] Barna reports that 79 percent of Americans accept female priests and pastors while only 39 percent of Evangelicals agree, as the Evangelical culture remains entrenched in complementarianism.[19] Many evangelical churches have a soft complementarian structure allowing women to lead while men hold

---

https://www.uua.org/re/tapestry/children/signs/session16/288929.shtml.

[15] York, "Antoinette Brown and Olympia Brown."

[16] Kimberly Ervin Alexander, and James P. Bowers, *What Women Want: Pentecostal Women Ministers Speak for Themselves* (Eugene, OR: Wipf & Stock Publishers, 2018), 109.

[17] Robert Jamieson, A. R. Fausset, and David Brown, *The Old Testament: From Song of Solomon to Malachi*, vol. 2 of *Commentary Critical and Explanatory on the Whole Bible* (Oak Harbor, WA: Logos Research Systems, Inc., 1997), 474-5.

[18] Leah Payne, "Why Foursquare's Female Leaders Have It Harder Today," ChristianityToday.com, CT Women, May 29, 2019, accessed August 3, 2022, https://www.christianitytoday.com/ct/2019/may-web-only/foursquare-church-aimee-semple-mcpherson-tammy-dunahoo.html.

[19] Kinnaman, "What Americans Think about Women in Power."

power.[20] Evangelicals' "middle of the road" posture attempts to keep both sides concerning women in senior leadership roles content.[21] Several mainline denominations have had women in top positions, including churches affiliated with the evangelical movement.[22] Of mainline congregations, 99 percent ordain women, while non-mainline report that they ordain 44 percent.[23]

In 2022, The Foursquare Church reported that 9 percent of its churches have female senior pastors, while the national representation has increased to 13.97 percent in 2019.

In 2016, according to Kinnaman's Barna Group study, "What Americans Think about Women in Power," only 9 percent of Protestant pastors in the U.S. are female.[24] Although miniscule, this national statistic surpasses The Foursquare Church's representation of 7 percent (also in 2016).[25] Data from the institution's annual reports state a slight increase in female senior leadership within the church.[26] As a result, the following section of this chapter presents further assessment of the International Church of the Foursquare Gospel (ICFG), the Episcopal Church (EC), the Assemblies of God

---

[20] Heather Matthews, "Uncovering and Dismantling Barriers for Women Pastors," CBE International, February 3, 2022, accessed August 3, 2022, https://www.cbeinternational.org/resource/article/priscilla-papers-academic-journal/uncovering-and-dismantling-barriers-women.
[21] Matthews, "Uncovering and Dismantling Barriers for Women Pastors."
[22] Matthews, "Uncovering and Dismantling Barriers for Women Pastors."
[23] Matthews, "Uncovering and Dismantling Barriers for Women Pastors."
[24] Kinnaman, "What Americans Think about Women in Power."
[25] The Foursquare Church, "2017 Cabinet Report," accessed July 3, 2022, http://s3.amazonaws.com/foursquare-org/assets/Cabinet_2017_NCO_Report.pdf.
[26] "This is Foursquare: Cabinet Report 2022," 4.

(AG), the United Methodist Church (UMC), and the Presbyterian Church (PC-USA).

In 2022, The Foursquare Church reported that 9 percent of its churches have female senior pastors,[27] while the national representation has increased to 13.97 percent in 2019 (see Table 3 below).[28]

Table 3. Foursquare Cabinet Report[29]

2021 Foursquare by the Numbers	Current Information
Pentecostal Ethos	Salvation: 134,439 Holy Spirit Baptism: 6,472 Baptisms by water: 7,445 Healing: 21,362
Moderation	No evidence reported
Women in Senior Leadership	Females licensed: 2675 (39.1%) Senior Female leaders: 132 (9%)
Integrated Mission	No evidence reported
Indigenous Empowerment	68,500 churches in 150 countries, with 1700 in the U.S.

As of June 28, 2022, Foursquare reports a slight increase to 9.8 percent of female senior pastors leading in the United States. However, in the early years of The Foursquare Church, nearly half of its pastors were females. Leah Payne advocates that the trajectory of women holding the highest roles within the denomination changed when the founder's daughter, Roberta Semple, her assumed successor, was replaced by her son, Rolf McPherson.[30] A century

---

[27] "This is Foursquare: Cabinet Report 2022," 4.
[28] "Pastor Demographics and Statistics in the US," Zippia (The Career Expert), accessed August 10, 2022, https://www.zippia.com/pastor-jobs/demographics/.
[29] "This is Foursquare: Cabinet Report 2022," 3.
[30] Payne, "Why Foursquare's Female Leaders Have It Harder Today."

later, The Foursquare Church has yet to name a woman at the helm of its denomination.

Various denominations are making history concerning the inclusion of women in their critical roles of leadership.

> In 2006, Katharine Jefferts Schori was elected to serve a nine-year term as the presiding bishop of the Episcopal Church of the United States—she was the first woman to hold the position. As of July 1, 2019, six women had been elected as diocesan or suffragan bishops in the Episcopal Church that year—the most ever elected in one year in the church's history, according to the Episcopal News Service.[31]

The head of the church's office of pastoral development, Bishop Todd Ousley said, "[T]here has been 'a dance' between society's changing attitude toward women as leaders and the 'church's efforts or, at certain points, the church's resistance to making this shift.'"[32] In 2017, the Episcopal Church reports 33 percent female pastors.[33]

A century later, The Foursquare Church has
yet to name a woman at the helm
of its denomination.

In 2018, the United States Assemblies of God (AG) unanimously selected Donna Barrett to serve as the denomination's General Secretary, the first female executive in over one hundred years.[34] As

---

[31] Anna Oakes, "Amid Growth in Leadership, One-Fifth of U.S. Clergy Are Female," Watauga Democrat, March 1, 2020, accessed August 3, 2022, https://www.wataugademocrat.com/community/amid-growth-in-leadership-one-fifth-of-u-s-clergy-are-female/article_739b14a1-212a-5d06-b429-4d888a369255.html.

[32] Oakes, "Amid Growth in Leadership."

[33] Oakes, "Amid Growth in Leadership."

[34] Claudette Riley, "Assemblies of God Selects First Woman Executive in 100+ Years," News-Leader, April 30, 2018, accessed August 3, 2022,

of 2021, the Assemblies of God reports almost 13,000 churches in the United States with more than three million members.[35] Since 2008, the Assemblies of God has ordained, on average, five women per week.[36] As of August 5, 2022, the AG reports a record of 27.6 percent of their ministers are women.[37] Nonetheless, more than eighty years following the 1935 General Council decision to allow women full ministerial rights, female ministers continue to struggle with exclusion from higher authority roles. The denomination reports that most senior leadership roles continue to be dominated by men.[38]

In 2020, the United Methodist Church reported full-time female clergy at 32 percent.[39] Rather than having a single executive leader, the structure of the United Methodist Church consists of a General Conference, the Council of Bishops, and the Judicial Council, each

---

https://www.news-leader.com/story/news/local
/ozarks/now/2018/04/30/assemblies-god-selects-first-woman-executiveassemblies-god-hires-female-executive-first-time-100-yea/564494002/.

[35] Assemblies of God. "Statistics on the Assemblies of God (USA): Female Ministers 1977 through 2021." Accessed August 10, 2022. http://www.ag.org/About/Statistics.

[36] Hannah McClellan, "Assemblies of God Ordains Record Number of Women," News & Reporting (Christianity Today, August 5, 2022), accessed August 10, 2022, https://www.christianitytoday.com/news/2022/august/assemblies-god-ordain-women-record.html.

[37] McClellan, "Assemblies of God Ordains."

[38] Saehee H. Duran, "Intentional Male Allies/Advocates: How Male Leaders Can Successfully Champion Female Ministers in the Assemblies of God U.S.A.," (D.Min. proj., Southeastern University, Lakeland, FL, 2022), 55, FireScholars, accessed April 13, 2022, https://firescholars.seu.edu/dmin/23/.

[39] Magaela C. Bethune, "2020 Geographical Trends of Gender Disparities in Composition and Compensation for UMC Clergy," Resource UMC, accessed August 10, 2022, https://www.resourceumc.org/en/partners/gcsrw/home/content/2020-geographic-trends-of-gender-disparities-in-composition-and-compensation-for-umc-clergy.

playing a significant role in the church's life. Women are represented in each of the sectors of the UMC structure. The UMC reports, "In many ways the United Methodist Church has been a standard-bearer among Judeo-Christian faith communions in terms of full-inclusion of women in the life, ministry, and witness of the institutional church and its regional and local expressions."[40] Although the United Methodist Church reports full inclusion of female senior leaders, the denomination openly confesses that there are places that need more work within its institution concerning equality for women.[41] In 1980, Marjorie Matthews became the first female bishop in the United Methodist Church and the first American woman to hold the position of bishop in any major Christian denomination.[42]

In 2020, the United Methodist Church
reported full-time female clergy
at 32 percent.
—Magaela C. Bethune

As of 2019, the Presbyterian Church (USA) reported that women represented 38 percent of active ordained ministers, and that most

---

[40] The People of the United Methodist Church, "Book of Resolutions: Every Barrier Down: toward Full Embrace of All Women in Church and Society," The United Methodist Church, accessed August 27, 2022, http://www.umc.org/en/content/book-of-resolutions-every-barrier-down-toward-full-embrace-of-all-women-in-church-and-society. (From *The Book of Resolutions of The United Methodist Church*. Copyright © 2016 by The United Methodist Publishing House. Used by permission.)
[41] The People of the United Methodist Church, "Book of Resolutions."
[42] "Marjorie Matthews (1916-1986): The First Woman Elected a Bishop in the United Methodist Church—1980," The United Methodist Church (General Commission on Archives and History), accessed July 9, 2022, http://www.gcah.org/history/biographies/marjorie-matthews.

of their members are female.[43] The report continues, "Women are also more likely to hold part-time and temporary ministry positions or to be called to serve struggling churches."[44] Another feature of this report by the PCUSA related to the gender pay gap among Presbyterian ministers, showing the gap as wider than the national average due to the less desirable appointments (small, struggling churches that men refuse to accept) given to women versus those given to men.[45]

> As of 2019, the Presbyterian Church (USA) reported that women represented 38 percent of active ordained ministers, and that most of their members are female.
> —The Presbyterian Outlook

In 2021, the Presbyterian Church (USA) openly and honestly reported its findings from a PC(USA) Minister Survey: Discrimination, Opportunity, and Struggles of Leadership Report.[46] The survey exposed that 37 percent of respondents reported some form of discrimination or harassment with 58 percent of women reporting gender-based discrimination.[47] Statistics from this 2021

[43] The Presbyterian Outlook, "The Rise of Women in the Pulpit," The Presbyterian Outlook, accessed October 8, 2022, https://pres-outlook.org/2019/10/the-rise-of-women-in-the-pulpit.
[44] The Presbyterian Outlook, "The Rise of Women in the Pulpit."
[45] The Presbyterian Outlook, "The Rise of Women in the Pulpit."
[46] Sean Payne and Susan Barnett, "PC(USA) Minister Survey: Discrimination, Opportunity, and Struggles of Leadership Report," Presbyterian Mission Agency, 2021, accessed August 10, 2022, https://www.presbyterianmission.org/wp-content/uploads/Minister-Descrimination-Opportunity-and-Struggles-of-Leadership-Report-copy.pdf.
[47] Payne and Barnett, "PC(USA) Minister Survey," 17.

survey showed women as facing more struggles as leaders than men in every category, as indicated in Table 4 below:[48]

Table 4. PC(USA) Minister Survey: 2021 Discrimination Report

Category	*Men*	*Women*
Accepted as Authority	39 percent	13 percent
Inclusion by Other Leaders	28 percent	13 percent
Recognition for Leadership Abilities	28 percent	13 percent
Not Having Work Validated by Others	28 percent	12 percent
Marital Status	15 percent	4 percent
Offensive Comments	37 percent	8 percent
Loneliness	40 percent	22 percent
Low Pay	47 percent	21 percent
Surprised at What I Do	44 percent	14 percent

A 2016 PC(USA) study concerning ordained pastors projects that gender parity will not take place until 2027, which is seventy-one years after the approval of women's ordination.[49]

Of note, it appears that qualification is not the issue for attaining a leadership rather the discrimination is due to gender.

This section on female senior leadership within the church has demonstrated that women face numerous challenges when it comes to leading in the twenty-first century. Whether leading from Capitol Hill or the pulpit, women have an option—to accept or reject the hierarchical culture. Although women successfully led in the civil rights and education reform movements, they continue to be

---

[48] Payne and Barnett, PC(USA) Minister Survey, 27.
[49] "Gender and Leadership in the PC(USA)," Presbyterian Mission Agency, Summer 2016, accessed August 3, 2022, https://www.presbyterianmission.org/resource/gender-leadership-pcusa/.

outnumbered in the most prestigious roles.[50] Of note, it appears that qualification is not the issue for attaining a leadership rather the discrimination is due to gender.

The United Methodist Church and the Presbyterian Church USA were the first two Protestant Christian denominations to ordain women.[51] Women continue to be highly represented within these two institutions. The United Churches of Christ (UCC) and Unitarian Universalists (UU) report "overall numbers of clergywomen equating (50 percent) or greater compared to the numbers of clergymen."[52] The Foursquare Church and the Assemblies of God report at least one woman at the executive level of their organization, but not in the role of president.

> The Foursquare Church and the Assemblies of God report at least one woman at the executive level of their organization, but not in the role of president.

Despite an increase in the statistics regarding female senior leaders within the church, women find themselves continually overlooked for the topmost titles held within these institutions. "It's not personal," a statement heard by women more than once when

---

[50] Catherine Hill et al., "Barriers and Bias: The Status of Women in Leadership," American Association of University Women, accessed August 3, 2022, https://ww3.aauw.org/research/barriers-and-bias/ February 29, 2016. https://eric.ed.gov/?id=ED585546.
[51] David Masci, "The Divide over Ordaining Women," Pew Research Center, accessed May 30, 2020, https://www.pewresearch.org/fact-tank/2014/09/09/the-divide-over-ordaining-women.
[52] Campbell-Reed, "No Joke: Resisting the Culture of Disbelief," Eileen Campbell-Reed, May 9, 2020, accessed August 3, 2022, https://cdn.eileencampbellreed.org/wp-content/uploads/No_Joke_Campbell-Reed_Rev_4-25-2018_Submitted_Version.pdf, 33.

dialoguing about the role of women in the church. That statement usually comes from some well-intended white male attempting to assuage the pain inflicted when sharing a stance against women in leadership. "It's not personal," he says—but "it most certainly is."[53]

> "It's not personal," he says—
> but "it most certainly is."
> —Kimberly Ervin Alexander and James Bowers

The Hurdles Women Face

Women face many hurdles in society. Nevertheless, hurdles that come from within the church cause the greatest sense of betrayal. Women do not feel at liberty to use their gifts within the church due to discrimination, patriarchy, and misinterpretation of Scripture. The church was intended to thrive with males and females in equal partnership. The church, the family, and humanity suffer when the relationship between men and women are in conflict.

> Women do not feel at liberty to use their gifts within the church due to discrimination, patriarchy, and misinterpretation of Scripture.

Mindy Smith proposes a theory regarding the discrimination, exclusion, hurdles, hindrances, and struggles women must navigate to preach the name of Jesus. She submits that the issues' root is the misinterpretation of Scriptures disallowing women to use their

---

[53] Alexander and Bowers, *What Women Want*, 43-46.

voice.[54] Smith continues that women must fight for their place at the table, for God neither purposed nor intended them to be overlooked and ignored but to be considered effective and influential leaders vital to the church.[55] As a result of the misinterpretation of Scripture that Smith references, women—equally called by God—continue to experience exclusion, harassment, spiritual abuse, and discrimination.

As a result of the misinterpretation of Scripture that Smith references, women— equally called by God—continue to experience exclusion, harassment, spiritual abuse, and discrimination.

Women come up against corrosive obstacles to their leadership, as Campbell-Reed notes; four obstacles that undermine the well-being of ministers and the people and churches include the following:

> Many churches still treat women as novelties rather than as ministers learning a spiritual and professional practice. Women are more likely to serve smaller rural and suburban churches, putting them at greater distance from other clergywomen. Yet peers and mentors are needed for perspectives that normalize ministry and advice that supports both the mundane and critical moments arising in ministry. One of the most visible, yet unquestioned obstacles women face is the overwhelming attention to their image and how they are perceived, rather than how they embody the purpose of their work and calling. This kind of undertow comes in an endless stream of complaints about everything from the height of one's heels to the length of

---

[54] Mindy Smith, "Her Story: Forming a Woman's Voice in the Pulpit," Digital Commons @ George Fox University, 2018, accessed August 3, 2022, https://digitalcommons.georgefox.edu/dmin/246/.
[55] Smith, "Her Story."

one's sermon to the way a pastor parents her children. When any clergywoman, including the most accomplished and effective leaders, get dismissed because they are women.[56]

The destruction and limitations resulting from injustice within the church toward women are oftentimes felt whether the result of the spoken word or simply due to systemic realities in place. In addition to these obstacles, the section below describes several other hurdles that female ministers face both from within and outside of the local church setting.

> The destruction and limitations resulting from injustice within the church toward women are oftentimes felt whether the result of the spoken word or simply due to systemic realities in place.

Hostile Preaching

Hostile preaching presents the first obstacle. In 2018, according to Campbell-Reed, John Piper restated "his view that women should not only avoid the pastorate, but they should also be barred from becoming seminary professors."[57] He blamed egalitarianism as the root cause of the fall of powerful men in the wake of the #MeToo movement. As Mimi Haddad notes, the movement exposes the destructive forces of patriarchy entrenched in Christian theology and

---

[56] Campbell-Reed, "No Joke."
[57] Campbell-Reed, "No Joke." See John Piper, "Is There a Place for Female Professors at Seminary?" January 22, 2018 audio and transcript, Desiring God, accessed August 3, 2022, https://www.desiringgod.org/interviews/is-there-a-place-for-female-professors-at-seminary.

practices.[58] Many churches and denominations, including recent accusations against Bill Hybels, choosing to take his retirement six months early,[59] are affected by the movement.[60] Campbell-Reed describes expected reactions that emerged either supporting or opposing Piper, Hybels, and other Evangelical leaders' interpretation regarding 1 Timothy 2:12 concerning equality.[61] Women are standing up and articulating discrimination, sexual harassment, and abuse of various types both in the church and sanctioned by the church.[62] Piper's supposition represents the typical stereotype and backlash that female leaders wrestle with daily in a patriarchal culture.

Sexual Harassment

Secondly, sexual harassment is another hurdle women face. Women both in Mainline and Evangelical churches report experiences of harassment and abuse. As Campbell-Reed states, "Just because women are ordained and hired does not mean they are fully welcomed or freed from sexism in the church."[63] The Pew Research Center survey, "Sexual Harassment at Work in the Era of #MeToo," reports that Americans were more concerned about men getting away with sexual harassment (50 percent) than they were with female abusers being believed (46 percent).[64] According to the study, the

---

[58] Mimi Haddad, "International Women's Day and CBE," CBE International, March 10, 2022, accessed August 3, 2022, https://www.cbeinternational.org/resource/article/mutuality-blog-magazine/international-womens-day-and-cbe.

[59] "Willow Creek Promises Investigation amid New Allegations Against Bill Hybels," Christianity Today, April 21, 2019, accessed January 4, 2023, https://www.christianitytoday.com/news/2018/april/bill-hybels-willow-creek-promises-investigation-allegations.html.

[60] Campbell-Reed, "No Joke."

[61] Campbell-Reed, "No Joke."

[62] Campbell-Reed, "No Joke."

[63] Campbell-Reed, "No Joke."

[64] Nikki Graf, "Sexual Harassment at Work in the Era of #Metoo," Pew Research Center's Social & Demographic Trends Project, April 4, 2018,

increased focus of sexual harassment and assault that the #MeToo movement has caused produces mixed views. Fifty-one percent of the men surveyed reported that they felt unsure of how to interact with women in the workplace due to the sexual focus. On another question, 51 percent of men also reported that they did not feel that speaking out in support of women would make much difference in the workplace concerning opportunities.[65] In an attempt to right what is wrong, a patriarchal culture blames the woman for holding her offender accountable rather than celebrating her pursuit of justice, further punishing the victim by isolating and excluding her.

In an attempt to right what is wrong, a patriarchal culture blames the woman for holding her offender accountable rather than celebrating her pursuit of justice, further punishing the victim by isolating and excluding her.

Power Struggles

A third hurdle women face has to do with what various types of power struggles. First, statistics from the foregoing studies have demonstrated that women have neither access in the corporate world, politics, academia, nor church to the same extent as their male counterparts due to their lack of membership in what is known as the Boys' Club.[66] Liz Elting proposes that "The Boys' Club" does

---

accessed August 3, 2022, https://www.pewresearch.org/social-trends/2018/04/04/sexual-harassment-at-work-in-the-era-of-metoo.
[65] Graf, "Sexual Harassment at Work in the Era of #MeToo."
[66] The "Boys' Club" consists of "informal social network of male friendships. There are tremendous advantages to being a Club member: mentoring, support, and promotions from within. This clique traditionally operates in spaces where females do not typically gather, such as strip clubs, sports events, and saunas. See Liz Elting, "How to Navigate a Boys'

not exist by accident; rather, its intentionality of power is constructed to ensure certain persons rise to the top: someone who is "one of them."[67] One can compare this club to a brotherhood, or, as Floyd Rose—an African American Church of Christ minister—describes, comparing racist treatment of blacks to the sexist treatment of women in the church:

> Through the years, sexism, like racism, has given men the right to define, confine, and control women. We have determined what they are, what they can and cannot do, and where they could and could not go. We have created a brotherhood, which not only emphasizes the difference, but gives men the advantage based on that difference. There is a frightening parallel between how blacks have historically been treated by a white dominated society, and how women are treated by a male dominated church.[68]

Within the church, the Boys' Club culture, alongside the Billy Graham Rule (BGR),[69] has denied women the same privileges, mentorship, and opportunities as men. The Billy Graham Rule was established to maintain integrity within Graham's ministry.[70] The precedent for the "Modesto Manifesto" is as follows:

> In 1948, Billy Graham began a series of evangelistic meetings in Modesto, California, along with his ministry team, comprised of Cliff Barrows, George Beverly ("Bev") Shea and Grady Wilson. Through a series of conversations

---

Club Culture," Forbes (Forbes Magazine, July 30, 2018), https://www.forbes.com/sites/lizelting/2018/07/27/how-to-navigate-a-boys-club-culture/?sh=2630d18b4025.

[67] Elting "How to Navigate a Boy's Club Culture."

[68] Floyd E. Rose, *An Idea Whose Time Has Come* (Columbus, GA: Brentwood Christian Press, 2002), 18.

[69] Billy Graham, "What's 'the Billy Graham Rule'?," Billy Graham Evangelistic Association, July 23, 2019, accessed August 3, 2022, https://billygraham.org/story/the-modesto-manifesto-a-declaration-of-biblical-integrity/.

[70] Graham, "What's 'the Billy Graham Rule'?"

about ministry life and its challenges, the group met together in Modesto and resolved to uphold the highest standard of Biblical morality and integrity. Many pastors, ministries, parachurch organizations and individuals have been inspired over the decades to adopt these philosophies.[71]

Although the purpose of the manifesto was morality and integrity in the male members of Graham's organization, the boundaries had an impact on women that continues to echo and encourages the exclusion of women.

In addressing the issue of the BGR, Saehee Duran advocates that male mentees receive personal guidance on pursuing, planning, and executing their next leadership level while females are guided toward managing projects or attending meetings and conferences for greater exposure.[72] The consequences of exclusive networking as a result of the BGR proves devastating to a female's ability to position herself for top-tier leadership.[73]

There appears to be a parallel between the Boys' Club and those elevating themselves above others in the name of righteousness. Men in both scenarios intentionally exclude women. The Talmud contains a second-century prayer that Jewish men recite daily, thanking God for not making them a woman, a Gentile, or a slave.[74] The Gospel of Luke contains a parable where Jesus addresses those that assumed themselves "righteous and regarded others with

---

[71] Graham, What's 'the Billy Graham Rule'?"

[72] Duran, "Intentional Male Allies/Advocates," 68.

[73] Duran, "Intentional Male Allies/Advocates," 62.

[74] Eliezer Segal, "A Dubious Blessing," University of Calgary, accessed August 3, 2022, http://people.ucalgary.ca/~elsegal/Shokel/991021_DubiousBlessing.htm l. For text of morning prayer that mentions this, see *"Siddur Ashkenaz,* Weekday, *Shacharit,* Preparatory Prayers, Morning Blessings 2-4," *Sefaria,* accessed January 3, 2023, https://www.sefaria.org/sheets/119367?lang=bi.

contempt" (Luke 18:9-14). Both these examples show the diminishing of others in order to elevate one's status. Jesus shares a parable about those who look down on others. He weaves the account into the story of the Pharisee who prays, "God, I thank you that I am not like other people: thieves, rogues, adulterers, or even like this tax collector" (Luke 18:11).

What is achievable for the male is not achievable for the female.

Another aspect of power struggles has to do with the issue of the "stained-glass ceiling." According to Cyrus Schleifer and Amy D. Miller's research, women fit into the role of pastor as well as men; however, the barriers, the "stained-glass ceiling," and the penalty of marriage and motherhood continue to obstruct women.[75] The stained-glass ceiling is defined as having a goal in sight yet remaining unattainable.[76] What is achievable for the male is not achievable for the female. Eagly and Carli cite Carol Hymowitz and Timothy Schellhard, who suggest that what looks inaccessible from the glass ceiling is merely a labyrinth and having a birds-eye view of the various ways to achieve the goal is the technique for success.[77]

---

[75] Cyrus Schleifer and Amy D. Miller, "Occupational Gender Inequality among American Clergy, 1976-2016: Revisiting the Stained-Glass Ceiling," *Sociology of Religion* 78, no 4 (Winter, 2017): 387-410, https://www.proquest.com/scholarly-journals/occupational-gender-inequality-among-american/docview/2266356251/se-2?accountid=40702.

[76] Alice Eagly and Linda Carli, "Women and the Labyrinth of Leadership," Harvard Business Review, September 1, 2007, accessed August 3, 2022, https://hbr.org/2007/09/women-and-the-labyrinth-of-leadership. According to Early and Carli, this term was first introduced as the "Glass Ceiling" in 1986 by Carol Hymowitz and Timothy D. Schellhard, "The Glass Ceiling: Why Women Can't Seem to Break the Invisible Barrier That Blocks Them from the Top Jobs," *Wall Street Journal*, March 24, 1986, 61.

[77] Eagly and Carli, "Women and the Labyrinth of Leadership."

Awareness of these options to achieve one's goal allows for options to be woven into the journey arriving at the objective in a timelier fashion than if one was unaware of those options.

Fourth, sexism and social inequity are tools often used to acquire power. Within the church, sexism has dictated that ministry is the exclusive calling of the male.[78] This is evident in that religious gatherings tend to be led by men. Male-led religious institutions and their mistakes continue to echo in society with the Catholic Church's sexual abuse scandals concerning minors[79] and the Southern Baptist Convention's sexual-abuse cover-ups over the past twenty years.[80] The Foursquare Church is not immune to sexual harassment, spiritual abuse cases, sexism, social inequity, and neglecting oversight of power.[81]

"Power is a funny thing; it derives its legitimacy from group recognition and sustains itself by the threat of exclusion."
—Liz Elting

---

[78] Paul King Jewett, *Ordination of Women: An Essay on the Office of Christian Ministry* (Eugene, OR: Wipf & Stock Publishers, 2012), 102.
[79] "Americans See Catholic Clergy Sex Abuse as an Ongoing Problem," Pew Research Center's Religion & Public Life Project (Pew Research Center), May 30, 2020, accessed August 31, 2022, https://www.pewresearch.org/religion/2019/06/11/americans-see-catholic-clergy-sex-abuse-as-an-ongoing-problem/.
[80] Kate Shellnutt, "Justice Department Investigates Southern Baptist Convention over Abuse," News & Reporting (Christianity Today), August 12, 2022, accessed August 31, 2022, https://www.christianitytoday.com/news/2022/august/federal-investigation-southern-baptist-abuse-executive-comm.html.
[81] Daniel Silliman, "Foursquare Abuse Response Ignites Fight over Transparency," News & Reporting (Christianity Today, August 4, 2022), https://www.christianitytoday.com/news/2022/august/foursquare-abuse-transparency-ignite-grace-larkin-lpu.html.

Elting states, "Power is a funny thing; it derives its legitimacy from group recognition and sustains itself by the threat of exclusion."[82] This exclusion or social inequity is injustice. Campbell-Reed reports progressive Christians telling 'Preacher Girl' jokes while protesting movements where women seek justice.[83]

> Women attending religious institutions that have at times shown sexist behavior and policies report significantly worse self-rated health than those attending inclusive religious environments.

Patricia Homan and Amy Burdette discuss sexism in, "When Religion Hurts: Structural Sexism and Health in Religious Congregations."[84] Their study began with the foundational assumption that religious institutions prove beneficial for health and well-being. However, the results of their findings showed pervasive systemic gender inequality. Homan and Burdette understand systemic gender inequity as women being prohibited from serving (1) on governing boards and the lack of decision-making power, (2) in the head role (a barrier also referred to as "stained-glass ceiling"), and (3) in the main service, teaching in co-ed environments, and governing roles.[85] Women attending religious institutions that have at times shown sexist behavior and policies report significantly worse

---

[82] Elting, "How to Navigate."

[83] Campbell-Reed, "No Joke."

[84] Patricia Homan and Amy Burdette, "When Religion Hurts: Structural Sexism and Health in Religious Congregations," *American Sociological Review* 86, issue 2 (2021): 234-55, https://doi.org/10.1177/0003122421996686; podcast interview with Jaimee Panzarella, April 2021, Scribd, accessed August 12, 2022, https://www.scribd.com/podcast/501326895/American-Sociological-Review-When-Religion-Hurts-Structural-Sexism-and-Health-in-Religious-Congregations-Authors-Patricia-Homan-and-Amy-Burdette-d.

[85] Homan and Burdette, "When Religion Hurts."

self-rated health than those attending inclusive religious environments. Women attending congregations that have also demonstrated discrimination based on gender reported the same level of health as those who did not attend a religious institution.[86] Men report not being affected at all or only "a little" by attending a sexist religious institution.[87]

The findings of the study described in the Homan and Burdette article, "When Religions Hurts" are important to this project, but the information concerning its impact upon men was the most significant disclosure. If a male is unaffected by sexism in the church, the question becomes, "Why not?" If systemic sexism is typical in an institution where men are only slightly affected by its presence, the toxicity within the environment will not be confronted. As a result, a sense of hopelessness can impact the mental and even physical health of the women in the congregation.

Conclusion

Women in ministry leadership report similar experiences as women in the political, corporate, and academic sectors. Although statistics indicate that those in the secular workplace enjoy greater acceptance from society in their roles than women in the religious sector, the hindrances, harassment, and hostility reported exist in all sectors. Power struggles, exclusion, and social inequity remain, impacting women in the workforce, regardless of career choice.

Full inclusion of women in every area of ministry leadership must stand as the biblical response to questions concerning a woman's place within the Church. If The Foursquare Church implements ways to include women in these roles, it will align with God's intent for the Church.

---

[86] Homan and Burdette, "When Religion Hurts."
[87] Homan and Burdette, "When Religion Hurts."

Chapter 6

What *Should Be*: A Prophetic Vision for The Foursquare Church

Introduction

Thus far, this literature review has focused on the foundational support of women in The Foursquare Church, addressing statistical data presented from various denominations, higher education, politics, and corporate studies. The first two sections studied reports of women's experiences with discrimination and gender bias, the restricting effect of androcentric interpretation of Scripture, and the daily barriers and roadblocks women face. As Pearl Buck insightfully proposes,

> Sometimes the accusation is true. It cannot be denied that too many of our exceptional women are mannish, hard, ruthless, and without grace. But who can blame them? By the time woman has made her way as near to the top as she can against tradition, she has been so laughed at, so criticized, so heaped with contempt, both good-natured and ill, so soiled with the anger and envy of those less successful than she, both men and women, that she is often all that she is said to be. She could scarcely have survived otherwise unless she had been that true miracle of a woman so full of pure grace that she could have kept herself intact. But why make superhuman demands upon women that are not made

upon men? The average successful man is also selfish, arrogant, and hard, and nobody blames him for it.[1]

After Buck shared a personal experience with a male president of a college for women who was requesting her assistance to train, in his terminology, his "girls," he said, "It is my aim to educate women to be the partners of men."[2] To this, Buck replied: "But who, is educating men to be the partners of women?"[3] The partnership Buck describes can only take place with education for each other. She continues that it will be difficult because of the long education away from each other.[4]

One hundred years after its founding, a gap remains in The Foursquare Church of women holding executive roles, serving as the senior pastor, and receiving invitations to decision-making tables equal to men.

One hundred years after its founding, a gap remains in The Foursquare Church of women holding executive roles, serving as the senior pastor, and receiving invitations to decision-making tables equal to men. Statistics across various denominations, with the exclusion of The United Churches of Christ (UCC) and Unitarian Universalists (UU), report having 50 percent (or greater)

---

[1] Pearl S. Buck, *Of Men and Women: How to Be for Each Other* (New York: Open Road Integrated Media, 2017), 169. "Pearl S. Buck (1892–1973) was a bestselling and Nobel Prize-winning author of fiction and nonfiction, celebrated by critics and readers alike for her groundbreaking depictions of rural life in China. Her renowned novel *The Good Earth* (1931) received the Pulitzer Prize and the William Dean Howells Medal. For her body of work, Buck was awarded the 1938 Nobel Prize in Literature—the first American woman to have won this honor."
[2] Buck, *Of Men and Women*, 137.
[3] Buck, *Of Men and Women*, 137.
[4] Buck, *Of Men and Women*, 138.

clergywomen, which indicates that other denominations are experiencing the same trends.[5] Women continue to groan as polity and policy do not produce egalitarianism, though the denominations hold firm to the status quo.[6]

Perhaps the contribution of female leaders,
in accord with God's plan, could offer
something new and fresh as women
and men partner together for
Kingdom purposes.

The stance of these denominations contrasts with Scripture, for the Bible reveals the stories of bold, courageous, intelligent, and compassionate women leading with God's approval. Yet the Church continues to silence and oppress women. Hierarchy has changed women—as Buck states, seemingly minimizing their contributions to the Kingdom. Perhaps the contribution of female leaders, in accord with God's plan, could offer something new and fresh as women and men partner together for Kingdom purposes.

God-Ordained

Aimee Semple McPherson was chosen to steward The Foursquare Church as its founder, which infers that God, who appoints leaders, intended that appointment for The Foursquare Church to release and empower women.[7] Therefore, I assert, that if women had equality in the denomination, then the representation of female

---

[5] Campbell-Reed, "No Joke!"
[6] Campbell-Reed, "No Joke!"
[7] See Romans 13:1b.

senior leaders and credentialed women would be 50 percent and greater.[8]

Surely God intended something unique for The Foursquare Church by establishing it through a woman.

Over the past one hundred years, representation by women in leadership has fallen although there has been an increase in the past decade. Surely God intended something unique for The Foursquare Church by establishing it through a woman. However, having a female founder did not necessarily result in complete egalitarianism As Rebecca Merrill Groothius states, "… any function that requires a significant part of a person's identity to remain untouched and unutilized … cannot justifiably be deemed permanent, fitting, and God-ordained."[9] Truly this idea should exist as an essential component of its prophetic vision for The Foursquare Church in the future.

Females Championing Other Female Leaders

The existence of female equality lends health and wholeness to the institution. Therefore, a priority in The Foursquare Church, I argue, is to intentionally place qualified women in executive roles, as church planters, and in healthy churches to lead. Another aspect of vision for the future to achieve this goal is the imperative that female leaders advocate for other female leaders. As Rowan Thompson

---

[8] Were this the case, women would represent at the executive level at 50 percent or greater rather than 20 percent currently and pastor churches at 50 percent or greater compared to 9 percent; see "This is Foursquare: Cabinet Report 2022," 3.
[9] Rebecca Merrill Groothius, *Good News for Women: A Biblical Picture of Gender Equality.* Grand Rapids, MI: Baker Books, 1997, 86.

asserts, women can and must use their influence to serve as allies to other women because women understand the bias, the injustice, the exclusion, and the political challenges of climbing into top-tier leadership.[10] To reach a goal of 50 percent of female leaders in The Foursquare Church, women must mentor, sponsor, and advocate for other women.

> Another aspect of vision for the future to achieve this goal is the imperative that female leaders advocate for other female leaders.

The Lean In organization describes six ways women can champion other women:

(1) Make Sure Women's Ideas are Heard

(2) Challenge the Likeability Penalty

(3) Celebrate Women's Accomplishments

(4) Encourage Women to Go for It

(5) Give Women Direct Feedback

(6) Mentor and Sponsor Other Women[11]

Just as this type of championing by women for other women strengthens execution of the prophetic vision, men also play a significant role in establishing gender equity and parity within The Foursquare Church leadership, as the following section describes.

---

[10] Rowan M. Thompson, "Advancing Equity, Diversity, and Inclusion: A How-to-Guide," Physics Today, March 10, 2022, accessed August 31, 2022, https://doi.org/10.1063/PT.33.4921.

[11] "6 Ways That Women Can Champion Each Other at Work," Lean In, accessed August 16, 2022, https://leanin.org/tips/workplace-ally#!.

Male Leaders Being
Other-Focused

For men to be other-focused in terms of establishing gender equity and parity involves a focus on justice. As the prophet, Micah describes, God has called His people "to do justice and to love kindness and to walk humbly with your God" (Mic. 6:7-8).

For men to be other-focused in terms of
establishing gender equity and parity
involves a focus on justice.

There are two duties toward humanity—justice, or strict equity, and mercy.[12] Tolerance of errors in interpretation of Scripture concerning women that supports doctrine theologically damaging to half the Church, can no longer be tolerated. As men become "other-focused" having a greater concern for justice and walking out that justice by affirming women in ministry thus having a more egalitarian perspective, women will gain better opportunities and equality will become attainable. According to Mimi Haddad, "The church holds three distinct positions concerning women's value and scope of leadership."[13] The positions, she asserts, are a (1) patriarchal perspective—men and women are unequal in being as well as

---

[12] Andrew Robert Fausset, A. R. Fausset, and David Brown, *Jeremiah-Malachi*, vol. IV of *A* Commentary, Critical, Experimental, and Practical, on the Old and New Testaments, Logos Bible Software, accessed August 21, 2022, https://www.logos.com/product/169281/a-commentary-critical-experimental-and-practical-on-the-old-and-new-testaments-vol-iv-jeremiah-malachi, 694.

[13] Mimi R. Haddad, "Examples of Women's Leadership in the Old Testament and Church History," in *Women in Pentecostal and Charismatic Ministry: Informing A Dialogue on Gender, Church, and Ministry*, ed. Margaret English de Alminana and Lois E. Olena (Leiden: Brill, 2017), 59.

unequal in their function, (2) egalitarianism perspective—equal in being/equal in function, (3) complementarian perspective—equal in being/unequal in function.[14] Haddad claims that each perspective extends or limits female access to leadership.[15] Changes in the future of The Foursquare Church requires a paradigm shift in thinking toward egalitarianism as holy alignment. As Linda Rooney notes, real change to gender equity and parity entails not just visible modifications but an alteration in the entity's spirit that aligns with God's intent.[16]

Tolerance of errors in interpretation of Scripture concerning women that supports doctrine theologically damaging to half the Church, can no longer be tolerated.

A prophetic vision for the future requires that men in leadership roles within The Foursquare Church begin by recognizing this: exclusiveness diminishes God in people's eyes, but inclusiveness weakens patriarchy.

Increasing awareness of the practical steps to change one's behavior to facilitate inclusiveness, requires clear articulation of those steps. As a researcher advocating a prophetic vision for male and female leaders within The Foursquare Church, I offer the following ten steps to endorse equity: (1) dismantle sexist systems, (2) question unlimited authority, (3) collaborate with intentionality, (4) confront gender and power irregularities within the institution, (5) do not remain neutral; be an advocate, (6) confront misogyny, favoritism,

---

[14] Haddad, "Examples of Women's Leadership," 59.
[15] Haddad, "Examples of Women's Leadership," 59.
[16] Linda Romey, "It's Time to Find out Where Religious Life Can Go without Patriarchy," Global Sisters Report, January 18, 2022, https://www.globalsistersreport.org/news/religious-life/column/its-time-find-out-where-religious-life-can-go-without-patriarchy.

and discrimination, (7) promote cross-gender mentoring, (8) gain understanding by listening, (9) educate beginning with the Creation account of equality, and (10) mirror Jesus's continual support of women.

> Exclusiveness diminishes God in people's eyes, but inclusiveness weakens patriarchy.

Jesus, the ultimate advocate, selected women as the first witnesses of His resurrection and again, as His spokespersons delivering the good news to the male disciples (Matt. 28:10; John 20:17-18).[17] Another example of Jesus's attitude toward women is evident in the story of the sinful woman who anoints Jesus's feet (Mark 14:3-9). Thus, women were not only valued as Jesus did in the examples above, but were also chosen throughout Scripture as leaders, demonstrating that God does not require only male representations of himself.[18] He requires both males and females to serve as His representation whether leading or serving.

God-Approved

Approval requires evaluation, which Paul emphasizes in this exhortation to the Thessalonian church: "but, just as we have been approved by God to be entrusted with the message" (1 Thess. 2:4). Michael Martin interprets this text to state,

> The missionaries spoke not from any wrong motive but because God had approved them to be entrusted with the gospel. He chose them. He entrusted them with a message. Commissioned by God, they concerned themselves with

---

[17] Duran, "Intentional Male Allies/Advocates," 48.
[18] Rebecca Merrill Groothuis, *Women Caught in the Conflict: The Culture War between Traditionalism and Feminism* (Eugene, OR: WIPF & Stock Publishers, 1997), 107.

pleasing the God who sent them with his message. For it was God who judged them trustworthy to carry his gospel, the same God who continued to judge their words, their actions, and their very hearts. A person obligated to speak for one who can judge the heart would be foolish to change the message in order to please the hearers. Such an act would comprise a breach of trust.[19]

In other words, those whom God chooses, He entrusts them to teach the gospel, take responsibility and be accountable to teach sound doctrine.

As Mathew Avery Sutton asserts, although Aimee Semple McPherson never joined any feminist organization, she was intentional in advocating for equality, which challenged patriarchy. One way to reach that goal, he continues, is McPherson's strategy of empowering women through education.[20] In February 1923, she established LIFE (Lighthouse of International Foursquare Evangelism) to equip men and women for the work of the ministry. That vision to educate both genders must remain a target for this denomination.

Conclusion

One hundred years after a woman founded The Foursquare Church there is a distinct difference in the number of women in leadership versus men in leadership. Of note however, is that this disparity is not unique, and is true of other denominations, excluding The United Churches of Christ and Unitarian Universalists. But does this commonality endorse biblical guidelines for leadership? As Part Two

---

[19] D. Michael Martin, *1, 2 Thessalonians*, vol. 33 of *New American Commentary* (Nashville, TN: Broadman & Holman Publishers, 1995), 73-74.

[20] Matthew Avery Sutton, *Aimee Semple McPherson and the Resurrection of Christian America* (Cambridge, MA; London, England: Harvard University Press, 2009), 206.

has proffered, the inequity is contra Scripture, and the Church must align with cultural norms for women in leadership positions.

Aimee Semple McPherson demonstrates
God's intent for women to have access to
the highest levels of leadership
within the institution.

Aimee Semple McPherson demonstrates God's intent for women to have access to the highest levels of leadership within the institution. Contra to societal norms, McPherson founds a denomination, starts a radio station, begins a four-year college, and travels across the United States as an evangelist. Her boldness and influence demonstrate that God affirms, appoints, and anoints female leaders, as it is also evident in the Bible.

Conclusion to Part Two

In the U.S., women holding executive roles in the corporate world, politics, and higher education are underrepresented, which is also true for senior female pastors. Despite the debate over the ability of women to lead, advances are evident that women are making strides in these arenas to dismantle the wall of patriarchy. The challenge remains, however, for The Foursquare Church, which has only seen a minimal increase statistically in senior female leadership since its inception.

Despite the debate over the ability of
women to lead, advances are evident.

From the beginning, The Foursquare Church has supported women; in fact, during the life of McPherson, 44 percent of senior pastors were women. Today, however, The Foursquare Church reports only 9 percent of its senior pastors as women. In Karen Tremper's study concerning credentialed women in the institution, she suggests, "The denomination is not as women-friendly as the theology might suggest."[21] Nonetheless, The Foursquare Church has an opportunity to revise the appearance and encourage female appointments to leadership roles. As John Stott states, "Without any fuss or publicity Jesus terminated the curse of the fall, reinvested woman with her partially lost nobility and reclaimed for his new kingdom community the original creation blessing of sexual equality."[22] Jesus reversed what sin created. Is then, The Foursquare Church aligning with Scripture in its theology and practice? This is a question that Part Three will address.

Jesus reversed what sin created.

Part Three focuses on the methodology for researching the experiences of five female leaders in the Foursquare denomination using surveys and interviews. The five women have a combined service in The Foursquare Church of almost 100 years. Their perceptions will contribute to the conversation about the representation of females in the denomination's leadership through their personal experience and historical context.

---

[21] Tremper, "Credentialed Women in the Foursquare Church: An Exploration of Opportunities and Hindrances in Leadership" (PhD diss., Fuller Theological Seminary, 2013), 187.
[22] John Stott, *Issues Facing Christians Today*, 4th ed. (Grand Rapids, MI: Zondervan, 2006), 482-533.

PART THREE

In the past seventy years (since the death of its female founder), The Foursquare Church has experienced a drastic decline in the number of women in leadership. Therefore, this phenomenological study explores the experiences of five female senior leaders in The Foursquare Church to evaluate potential reasons for the decline in females serving in leadership roles in the denomination.

Chapter 7

The Research Methodology

Research Questions

The main question in this research project was, "In a denomination, founded by a woman, why are women underrepresented at the senior leadership level?" A second question is, Are there commonalities in their experiences and perceptions regarding the decline in female representation at senior leadership levels?"

Preparation of the Project

Part One of this book examined the biblical-theological foundation for including (or excluding) women in leadership. Part Two identified statistics and barriers pertaining to the role of women in sacred and secular leadership. These two portions of the book provide the context for participant research—the focus of Part Three.

John W. Creswell and J. David Creswell in *Research Design* present three methodologies, which are: qualitative, quantitative, and mixed methods.[1] The qualitative methodology is an exploration to understand the experiences and perceptions of individual and/or groups.[2] The qualitative research method involves open-ended

---

[1] John W. Creswell and J. David Creswell, *Research Design: Qualitative, Quantitative, and Mixed Methods Approaches*, 5th ed. (Thousand Oaks, CA: SAGE Publications, Inc., 2018), 3.
[2] Creswell and Creswell, *Research Design*, 4.

questions and procedures, collecting data in the participants' setting, and analyzing the data inductively.[3] Carol Roberts and Laura Hyatt suggest using this technique when–an in-depth investigation of the essence of shared experience and individual perspectives is the project's target.[4] Quantitative methodology tests objective theory by examining the relationships among variables. I measure these variables using various instruments analyzing numbered data with statistical procedures.[5] Creswell and Creswell suggest this technique when the goal is to quantify a problem; they report that the quantitative method is more scientific and objective, allowing numerical certainty. This technique removes any bias allowing me to analyze the data only based on numerical findings. Creswell and Creswell's third approach is called mixed methods. This approach combines qualitative and quantitative data in response to the research questions.[6]

By investigating the individual encounters and experiences of the five participants (through a prefacing survey and interviews), I gained a more thorough understanding of their experiences. A qualitative approach was chosen as it offers an opportunity to study the phenomenon (i.e., experiences as female senior leaders).[7]

John Creswell and Cheryl Poth provide five approaches to data collection activity. This project utilized the phenomenology approach as defined by the authors:

---

[3] Creswell and Creswell, *Research Design,* 4.
[4] Carol Roberts and Laura Hyatt, *The Dissertation Journey: A Practical and Comprehensive Guide to Planning Writing, and Defending Your Dissertation* (Thousand Oaks, CA: Corwin, 2019), 143.
[5] Roberts and Hyatt, *The Dissertation Journey,* 7.
[6] Creswell and Creswell, *Research Design,* 4.
[7] John W. Creswell and Cheryl N. Poth, *Qualitative Inquiry & Research Design: Choosing among Five Approaches,* 4th ed. (Los Angeles, CA: SAGE, 2018), 79.

1. Multiple individuals who have experienced the phenomenon

2. Finding people who have experienced the phenomenon

3. Finding individuals who have experienced the phenomenon, a criterion sample

4. Interviews with a range of people (e.g., five to twenty-five)

5. Interviews, often multiple interviews with the same individual

6. Bracketing one's experiences, logistics of interviewing

7. Transcriptions, digital files[8]

Two venues served to acquire data for this project. The first is a survey through SurveyMonkey. The second is a sixty to ninety-minute interview through Zoom. This method allowed me to make observations and conduct in-depth, open-ended, or semi-structured interviews. In addition, the naturalistic inquiry[9] allowed me to observe, describe, and interpret the interviewees' actions and behaviors throughout the conversation.

As a female, ordained minister in The Foursquare Church, I had a potential bias. I have served in various capacities for over a decade and has interest in contributing to the study concerning the lack of female representation within the denomination. I also had a relationship with several participants. My project advisor was aware of my relationship with the institution and the participants and worked with me to maintain integrity in this study.

---

[8] Creswell and Poth, *Qualitative Inquiry,* 150.
[9] J. Armstrong, "Naturalistic Inquiry," in *Encyclopedia of Research Design,* ed. N. J. Salkind (Newbury Park, CA: SAGE Publications, Inc., 2010), 1037, https://dx.doi.org/10.4135/9781412961288.n262

The Foursquare Church reports 2,807 female leaders within the denomination; this number includes 132 senior pastors in the United States.[10] Of the 132 female senior pastors, this phenomenological study investigated five. The selection size was small since the methodology used in this research was qualitative. The small sampling size was due to the depth and breadth of the data collection.

Of the 132 female senior pastors, this phenomenological study investigated five.

The participants are ordained female ministers, actively serving in a senior leadership capacity in The Foursquare Church in the United States. For this study, the phrase "female senior leader" refers to a senior pastor, co-senior pastor, or executive leader. In addition, the participants had to be willing to dialogue with me concerning personal pastoral experiences. I chose participants who varied in age, role, and demographic. The five leaders understood the problem of the study and the research questions.

Instruments Used in Data Collection

As suggested by Roberts and Hyatt, the data collection process was initiated by determining a data collection plan. I set up a data source chart to track who received the instrument, when they received the instrument, and who completed it.[11] This method of organization assisted in efficiently following the process of data collection.

The data was gathered through an Internet-based company, SurveyMonkey, which hosted and emailed the surveys to the participants. I created the survey by aligning the fifteen questions

---

[10] "This is Foursquare: Cabinet Report 2022," 3.
[11] Roberts and Hyatt, *The Dissertation Journey*, 152.

with the project's research questions. The survey included fifteen strategic, closed-ended questions that would assist in answering the research question: "In a denomination founded by a woman, why are women underrepresented at the senior leadership level?" and the second question, "Are there commonalities in their experiences and perceptions regarding the decline in female representation at senior leadership levels?" Once participants completed and returned the surveys, I kept the information private and stored in a password-protected computer. I am the only individual with access to the participant's information.

Upon receipt of the surveys, I scheduled a sixty- to ninety-minute interview with each participant through Zoom. Approval for recording the interview was received from the participants prior to beginning the session. After the interviews were completed, I transcribed the interviews looking for patterns, similarities, and repeated verbiage.

The construction of the survey included four segments. The initial five questions pertained to demographics (See Table 5 below).

Table 5. Demographic Data

Question 1	Question 2	Question 3	Question 4	Question 5
What is your title in your church (current or previous)	How long did/have you served in the above-mentioned leadership role?	Marital Status during the above-referenced leadership assignment?	Did you have children during the above-referenced leadership period?	Which of the following describes your primary duty in the church?

The response options for the first five questions in the survey include the following:

- Question 1
    - Senior or lead pastor
    - Co-senior or co-lead (with my spouse)
    - Co-senior or co-lead pastor (with a male counterpart)
    - Co-senior or co-lead pastor (with another woman)
    - Other
- Question 2
    - 0 to 5 years
    - More than 5 years but less than 10 years
    - More than 10 but less than 15 years
    - More than 15 years
- Question 3
    - Single
    - Married
    - Divorced
    - Widowed
- Question 4
    - Yes
    - No
- Question 5
    - Preaching
    - Teaching Bible Studies
    - Women Ministry Leader
    - Children or Youth Ministry Leader
    - Pastoral Counselor
    - Missions Pastor
    - Other

The second portion of the survey contains three questions tracking the participant's emotional responses to their experiences within the institution (See Table 6 below).

Table 6. Emotional Response

Question 6	Question 7	Question 8
To what extent have you felt affirmed within the district where you serve The Foursquare Church?	To what extent have you felt affirmed among your peers within The Foursquare Church?	To what extent have you felt affirmed from the national level of The Foursquare Church?

The response options for questions 6-8 in the survey include the following:

- Question 6
  - Not at All
  - Very Little
  - Somewhat
  - To a Good Extent
  - To a Great Extent
- Question 7
  - Not at All
  - Very Little
  - Somewhat
  - To a Good Extent
  - To a Great Extent
- Question 8
  - Not at All
  - Very Little
  - Somewhat
  - To a Good Extent
  - To a Great Extent

The third segment was comprised of five questions regarding the participant's practical experiences. (See Table 7 below).

Table 7. Practical Experience

Question 9	Question 10	Question 11	Question 12	Question 13
To what extent have you experienced upward mobility/ advancement in ministry as your male counterparts?	To what extent has Foursquare met your expectations as a support system to aid in leadership growth through coaching?	As a female senior leader, at what extent do you feel included in the community of The Foursquare Church?	To what extent do you feel that Foursquare empowers women in key roles within its denomination?	To what extent do you agree that opportunities to preach, to lead, and to hold executive office in the denomination given to The Foursquare Founder, are available to you?

The response options for questions 9-13 in the survey include the following:

- Question 9
  - Not at All
  - Very Little
  - Somewhat
  - To a Good Extent
  - To a Great Extent
- Question 10
  - Not at All
  - Very Little
  - Somewhat
  - To a Good Extent
  - To a Great Extent
- Question 11
  - Not at All
  - Very Little
  - Somewhat

- o   To a Good Extent
- o   To a Great Extent
- Question 12
  - o   Not at All
  - o   Very Little
  - o   Somewhat
  - o   To a Good Extent
  - o   To a Great Extent
- Question 13
  - o   Not at All
  - o   Very Little
  - o   Somewhat
  - o   To a Good Extent
  - o   To a Great Extent

The fourth section contains two questions with a goal of ascertaining the personal response of each participant to their experience. See Table 8 below.

Table 8. Personal Response

Question 14	*Question 15*
To what extent do you feel your gender is limiting your call in The Foursquare Church?	To what extent are you likely to recommend the Foursquare denomination other female leaders seeking denominational affiliation and ministry leadership opportunities?

The response options for questions 14-15 in the survey include the following:

- Question 14
  - o   Not at All
  - o   Very Little
  - o   Somewhat
  - o   To a Good Extent
  - o   To a Great Extent
- Question 15
  - o   Not at All
  - o   Very Little

    o   Somewhat
    o   To a Good Extent
    o   To a Great Extent

The second method of data collection included interviews. This method allowed for follow-up questions from the survey to increase the depth of the participants' responses. The interview method allowed me to become the primary instrument, i.e., the one participating, creating the survey, selecting the participants, interviewing, note taking, observing, and analyzing the data to determine the phenomenon being studied.

> I was intentional in maintaining objectivity
> by allowing the participant to share her
> experience and asking pertinent questions.

I was intentional in maintaining objectivity by allowing the participant to share her experience and asking pertinent questions. A one-on-one dialogue through Zoom with each of the five interviewees was scheduled and conducted in sixty-to ninety-minute uninterrupted meetings. All five participants agreed to have the interview recorded, and the recorded sessions are currently held on a password-protected computer.

Data Collection—Surveys

Over ten weeks, I collected data from two platforms—online surveys and face-to-face interviews through Zoom. The survey responses allowed me to direct the interview questions toward the individual participants. This approach allowed for further understanding based on the participants' years of experience.

Question 1: What is your title in your church (current or previous)? Forty percent of the participants responded with senior or lead pastors, 40 percent with other, and 20 percent with co-senior or co-lead (with their spouse).

Question 2: How long did/have you served in the above-mentioned leadership role? Sixty percent of the participants have served The Foursquare Church for more than fifteen years.

Question 3: What was your marital status during the above referenced leadership assignment? Eighty percent of the participants were married during the referenced time of leadership.

Question 4: Did you have children during the above referenced leadership period? Sixty percent of the participants were parents of young children during the referenced leadership period.

Question 5: Which of the following describes your primary duty in the church? Sixty percent reported "other" as their primary duty, 20 percent selected "preaching," and 20 percent reported "pastoral counseling" as their primary duty.

Question 6: To what extent have you felt affirmed within the district where you serve The Foursquare Church? Sixty percent of the participants felt affirmed "to a great extent" within their district, 20 percent reported to a "good extent," and 20 percent reported "very little."

Question 7: To what extent have you felt affirmed among your peers within The Foursquare Church? Forty percent felt affirmed "to a great extent," 40 percent reported to a "good extent," and 20 percent reported "very little."

Question 8: To what extent have you felt affirmed from the national level of The Foursquare Church? Forty percent reported they felt affirmed "to a great extent," 20 percent reported "to a good extent," 20 percent reported "somewhat," and 20 percent reported, "not at all."

Question 9: To what extent have you experienced upward mobility/ advancement in ministry as your male counterparts? Twenty percent reported "not at all," 20 percent felt "somewhat," 40 percent felt "to a good extent," 20 percent reported, "to a great extent."

Question 10: To what extent has Foursquare met your expectations as a support system to aid in leadership growth through coaching? Sixty percent of the participants reported "very little," 20 percent reported "to a good extent," and 20 percent "to a great extent."

Question 11: As a female senior leader, to what extent do you feel included in the community of The Foursquare Church? Forty percent felt included "somewhat," 40 percent felt "to a good extent" and 20 percent reported, "to a great extent."

Question 12: To what extent do you feel Foursquare empowers women in key roles within its denomination? Twenty percent reported "very little," 60 percent reported "somewhat," and 20 percent "to a good extent."

Question 13: To what extent do you agree that opportunities to preach, lead, and hold executive office in the denomination given to the Foursquare Founder, are available to you? Twenty percent of the participants reported "not at all," 60 percent "to a good extent," and 20 percent, "to a great extent."

Question 14: To what extent do you feel your gender is limiting your call in The Foursquare Church? Twenty percent reported "not at all," 40 percent said, "very little," and 40 percent reported "somewhat."

Question 15: To what extent are you likely to recommend the Foursquare denomination to other leaders seeking denominational affiliation and ministry leadership opportunities? Twenty percent selected, "somewhat," 40 percent, "to a good extent," and 40 percent reported, "to a great extent."

Data Collection—Interviews

All five interviewees, female senior leaders concerned about the issues within this project, spoke with transparence in their discussions with me. They each demonstrated integrity in the interview process with the information shared, hopeful that change might occur due to the project. The leaders were vulnerable, exposing history and agreeable to going on record with their experiences. The environment was safe, and countless emotions occurred during the interviews. Together the participants have provided over a century of service to The Foursquare Church.

Confidential information was shared during the sixty- to ninety-minute interview process. I carefully selected the data included in this write-up to maintain the confidentiality of the interviewees. Therefore, some of the information will not be included but will remain in my safe care on a password-protected computer for five years. Other information may be shared in chapter 9 of this book found in "quotations only," to protect the participant's confidentiality.[12]

All five interviewees, female senior leaders
concerned about the issues within this
project, spoke with transparence in
their discussions with me.

Participant A began the dialogue with, "The women are more of the problem than you realize. Many are wrestling with their theology concerning women and their roles all based on what has been poured into them." Fathers, spouses, and other male figures have all contributed to the theology that women hold. Having this understanding, many women do not respond favorably when God

---

[12] See Appendix B, "Participant Interview Responses."

calls them into ministry. She continues, "However, our denomination has no lack of female leaders. The women are trained and developed just as are the men. The men need training concerning women and their place within the denomination. Women often feel they are not invited to the decision-making table. Men also feel uninvited, unheard, or given opportunities."

When Participant A was asked about "the glass ceiling" within the denomination, her response was, "I do not feel we have a glass ceiling in our denomination; we have a glass floor. The problem is not corporate. The problem is not in our bylaws or our governance. Our problem is not our willingness to appoint a woman to a specific role. It is on the ground floor. Generally, people do not know how to raise leaders (male or female)."

When asked about hindrances to women in senior leadership roles and the underrepresentation in The Foursquare Church, she responded, "Discrimination within The Foursquare Church has been an issue for some time. In 1998, the president of the denomination took the platform in Tulsa, Oklahoma, and repented on behalf of The Foursquare Church for their behavior toward women and the exclusion of women in leadership roles." She explained, "Women were licensed and ordained under Aimee Semple McPherson, but under her son's leadership, they gave token licenses to women."

> "Women were licensed and ordained under Aimee Semple McPherson, but under her son's leadership, they gave token licenses to women."

She explained the difference in leadership between the founder and her son: "Rolf McPherson is the classic story of appointing someone with a similar anointing. He had an administrative anointing rather than a ministerial anointing, which was very limiting. Under his leadership, The Foursquare Church transitioned from being Spirit-led to administratively led." She does not feel that patriarchy exists at a high level within the denomination since a good balance of male and female representation currently exists in the boardroom. However, she agrees there continue to be pockets of patriarchy evident within the institution, and she described The Foursquare Church as inherently complementarian and not egalitarian.

Participant A mentioned that very few women are appointed in The Foursquare Church to churches of significant size. She claims that as a result, women are planting and growing churches from the ground up rather than waiting for a male leader or sponsor to offer them a healthy church. When asked about the underrepresentation of women compared to other denominations also ordaining women, her response was, "We might be low in numbers, but we are not zero."

When asked about the underrepresentation of women compared to other denominations also ordaining women, her response was, "We might be low in numbers, but we are not zero."

Participant A shared the complex pathway women must navigate within The Foursquare Church toward senior leadership roles. She mentioned the segregation of male and female networking. Participant A has experienced or witnessed injustice, abuse, and bullying within the denomination on more than one occasion. Although there continues to be plenty of areas that need attention and direct oversight within The Foursquare Church, she is hopeful that the denomination will move forward as women stand up, use their voices, and take their rightful place. Her concluding statement was, "It begins with teaching the men."

Participant B shared the progression from being a congregational member to serving as a senior leader within The Foursquare Church. The conversation began with discussing the developmental process for female leaders.[13] Participant B responded, "One of the problems in The Foursquare Church is that no one is intentionally developing female leaders. There are programs available for mentoring women. However, a woman who has never seen or sat under the teaching of a female pastor does not have a role model and is reticent to enter a coaching or mentoring program. The potential [that a woman may have] to lead [in a various position such as overseeing greeters] and the call of God on a person's life [to serve as a pastor/shepherd] are not the same things [sic]." Men are not developing women; they are developing men, she suggests. She believes that men do not have the skill set to train, support, and release women and must be educated in this area.

She believes that men do not have the skill set to train, support, and release women and must be educated in this area.

Participant B mentioned that during her time as a member, she only saw a woman preaching a few times in The Foursquare Church. She stresses that licensed women were unique, and those she witnessed in the past serving were doing so in support roles; she witnessed no visual representation of female senior pastors. She said, "Women in The Foursquare Church are not even sure women can hold every role within The Foursquare Church because they have yet to see it."

---

[13] The developmental process this participant referred to has to do with her seeing a woman who has leadership potential and therefore mentoring and training that woman to help her develop various leadership skills.

Participant B feels that the difficulty The Foursquare Church is currently facing regarding female underrepresentation began with injustices concerning women and licensure. She said, "I do not believe that when men were being licensed early on, they were asked about their theology concerning female pastors. This is part of the problem in our denomination. It was assumed that since the denomination had a female founder, they affirmed women in lead roles. Now, they are backtracking to repair the damage. Today, licensees are asked about their stance concerning women and are refused a license if they disagree with the egalitarian stand in The Foursquare Church. We must do better in appointing, licensing, and accountability."

Participant B revealed her concern about the current allegations of abuse and harassment in The Foursquare Church. She said, "Repentance equals change of direction. Although there appears to be deep repentance concerning the stories that came out at Connection [2022], these stories cannot be ignored. Something other than "I am sorry for what happened" is necessary. Admit wrong. Admit neglect. Then, there should be fruit following the words." She continued with great conviction that women must feel spiritually and physically safe within our churches. She then asked, "What are the common denominators of abuse cases within our denomination? We must look for that!"

She said, "Women in The Foursquare Church are not even sure women can hold every role within The Foursquare Church because they have yet to see it."

Participant B feels strongly that there is a problem between potential leaders and licensing approvals. She is concerned that women continue to be "tokens" within the denomination carrying the weight of the responsibility without the call. With the underrepresentation of women in senior leadership roles within The Foursquare Church, licensing more women that are not called, trained, or prepared is not the answer for the sake of statistics.

When asked what is or has The Foursquare Church done to better prepare you for other leadership roles within the church, her response was, "Nothing. Other women have helped me, have invited me to the table, and have championed me but not the institution." She concluded the conversation with, "If you say I am valuable and influential, let me be."

Participant C began the interview by describing two or three male sponsors or champions during her journey within The Foursquare Church. She described the male leaders as sensitive to the "temperature in the room" and countered by surrounding her with support. She recalls on several occasions feeling or being silenced in the room. She stated, "I keep hearing the denomination is not ready for a woman at the helm." (She was referring to the 2019 Presidential election in which Tammy Dunahoo lost to a male.) She said, "How can it be that after nearly a century, there has not been a qualified woman for the lead role of The Foursquare Church?" She argues there are plenty of well-prepared women in The Foursquare Church. She proposes that there is no lack of training for women within the institution and that God is raising women at alarming rates.

She said, "How can it be that after nearly a century, there has not been a qualified woman for the lead role of The Foursquare Church?"

When asked about hindrances to women in the institution, she said, "Aimee Semple McPherson was silenced and controlled nearing the end of her ministry by her manager. As a result, her children had to ask permission to visit her. I believe this controlling relationship impacted the denomination and possibly [also had an impact] upon her son."

Participant C mentioned the house model church and claimed that women flock to this method. Without support and financial resources, the house-model method is attractive to many women who feel called yet unsupported by the institution. The conversation closed with, "The Foursquare Church is not the same as it was when Aimee was at the helm."

Participant D began the interview by describing an environment where men were invited to dialogue at the table. In the same meeting, the women and pastors' wives were ushered out of the room for lunch and shopping. Participant D, although a lead pastor, was not invited to the meeting.

The conversation closed with, "The Foursquare Church is not the same as it was when Aimee was at the helm."

When asked about the support for female leaders, based on her experience, she responded, "I do not look to the denomination for affirmation. The denomination is no more than a legal covering, and that is all. I have received helpful tools from individuals over the years, but none from the institution. Eventually, you will be disposed of." She said, "Do not give your heart to an organization. Give your heart to people."

She said, "Do not give your heart to an organization. Give your heart to people."

When I asked about her experience with discrimination or hindrances as a senior female leader, she responded, "Rolf McPherson came into the denomination and was extremely conservative, controlling, and heavy-handed. The denomination could be described as, "older white men in charge." The participant feels that the shift when Rolf McPherson superseded its founder continues to plague the institution.

Participant D was open and honest about her experiences within the institution. She did not share any hope of change in the future concerning women and their roles. She reported that The Foursquare Church was supportive in theory but not in practice. Finally, this participant spoke of being wounded and the lack of response by the denomination.

Participant E shared her experience of struggles and frustration while serving as a senior leader. She reported that no real encouragement exists for women and that pastors' wives receive more recognition than female pastors; and while the role of pastor's wife is *normal,* the role of female pastor is not. Although the denomination supports women on paper, on multiple occasions, Participant E heard, "Oh, so you are the token."

Participant E addressed the spiritual abuse cases that The Foursquare Church is currently facing. She said, "Victims of spiritual abuse experience the same type of trauma as rape victims. We should take it as seriously as we do rape." She fears the institution is not taking the allegations seriously. As a seasoned leader, she reports seeing many women leave The Foursquare Church wounded. When the participant was asked to elaborate, she responded, "Whenever Rolf McPherson replaced our founder, a spirit of control was brought into the denomination, and in my opinion, that same control over women is active today." She said, "We have lost an entire generation of women. I have watched them come and go." She also mentioned that the denomination does not respect women's education although the women are frequently the most educated in the room.

She said, "We have lost an entire generation of women. I have watched them come and go."

I asked Participant E if she felt women had the same opportunities as the founder. She responded, "Absolutely not. Women plant churches today because the institution is unlikely to appoint them to a healthy church." She explained that the healthier, larger churches are appointed to men while women are encouraged to plant churches. In her opinion, women who plant churches are set up to fail as the institution does not support the church plants with resources. When asked about her opportunities compared to the founder, she said, "I am not related to anyone within the denomination, so I don't get the same opportunities others might." She said, "Nepotism is alive and well within the denomination."

During the interview, the participant wept.

During the interview, the participant wept. After several decades of service in various roles throughout the denomination, the injustice and continual rejection are felt deeply in this participant. Her final statement was, "The face of the church has to change. We are no longer making disciples; that should be the focus."

Chapter 8

Survey and Interview Results

The online survey was finalized by each of the participants completing the fifteen questions.[1] The inquiries with the highest percentages were as follows:

The first category of the survey provided demographic information. Forty percent of the participants were senior or lead pastors, with 40 percent selecting "other" as their current role in the church. Sixty percent of the participants have served in The Foursquare Church for more than fifteen years. Eighty percent were married, and 60 percent had children while fulfilling their roles. When asked, "Which of the following describe your primary duty in the church?" Again, 60 percent of the participants reported "other" as their primary duty in the church.

The second category, the emotional response, gave insight into how they "felt" being a leader in The Foursquare Church. Sixty percent of the participants reported they felt affirmed within the districts where they serve "to a great extent." Forty percent of the participants reported they felt affirmed to a "good extent," and 40 percent, "to a great extent." When asked, "To what extent do you feel affirmed from the national level of The Foursquare Church?" Forty percent reported, "to a great extent."

In category three, practical experience, when asked, "To what extent have you experienced upward mobility/advancement in ministry as

---

[1] See Appendix C, "Survey Results in Graph Format."

your male counterparts?" 40 percent answered, to a good extent. Twenty percent were reported in each of the following three categories: "to a good extent," "somewhat," and "not at all."

When asked, "To what extent has Foursquare met your expectations as a support system to aid in leadership growth through coaching, 60 percent reported "very little," and 40 percent reported "somewhat" or "to a good extent" when asked if they felt included in the community of The Foursquare Church.

Regarding a question whether respondents felt The Foursquare Church empowers women in key roles within the institution, 60 percent reported that they felt The Foursquare Church does do so.

In response to the question whether The Foursquare Church gives women ministers today the same opportunities as given to the Foursquare founder, 60 percent responded, "to a good extent" that those opportunities were also available.

The outcomes of the final category, personal response, allowed them to delve a bit deeper into their experiences and realities while leading in The Foursquare Church. For example, when asked, "Do you feel your gender limits your call in The Foursquare Church?" 40 percent of the participants reported "very little," and 40 percent felt "somewhat."

Regarding the interview results, on multiple occasions, I read the transcriptions, listened to the interviews, and immersed herself in the details of the participants' responses. As a result, categories, themes, and patterns became evident.[2] The five participants in this study are influential female leaders within The Foursquare Church, in this study the women shared their opinions, perspectives, and experiences while serving in the institution.

---

[2] Roberts and Hyatt, *The Dissertation Journey,* 168.

The survey was divided into four segments to lay a foundation for the interview using the same divisions—demographic data, emotional response, practical experience, ad personal response. The tables below identify the results.

Table 9. Demographic Data

Question 1 What is your title in the church?	Question 2 How long have you served in the role?	Question 3 Marital Status	Question 4 Did you have children during the time of service?	Question 5 What are your primary duties?
60 percent are lead or co-lead pastors	Greater than fifteen years	80 percent are married	60 percent reported having children	60 percent reported other

Most of the participants in this project are lead or co-lead senior pastors, married with children, perform duties described as "other," and have over fifteen years of experience within The Foursquare Church.

Table 10. Emotional Response

Questions (6-8)	Key Words from the question	Main Points from Conversations	Elaboration	Key Words/Phrases Used
To what extent do you feel affirmed in your district, among your peers, and from the national level?	Affirmation	Words are essential, but actions must follow.	"I have been given room at decision-making tables."	Encouraged by peers
		Affirmation is found in relationships, not in institutions.	"I planted a church when that was the only choice for women in the denomination. Men were not placing them."	Tokenism Discrimination The denomination does not affirm women; peers have encouraged me.
To what extent have you felt affirmed among your peers within The Foursquare Church?		A denomination founded by a woman, supposedly egalitarian, is so on paper only.	"After all these years of service, I feel like a nobody in the denomination."	I have been encouraged to use my voice. I have had no encouragement.
To what extent have you felt affirmed from the national level of The Foursquare Church?		No affirmation for women.	"I pay the annual licensing fee, and what do I get for that? No support, no encouragement, nothing." "No affirmation within my district."	I feel the current executive team champions women. Injustice Inequality I have a place at the table.

Table 11. Practical Experience

Questions 9-13	Key Concepts	Main Points	Elaboration	Key Words Used
To what extent...- have you experienced an upward mobility like your male counterparts? *Has Foursquare met your expectations for growth?* *Has Foursquare included you?* *Has Foursquare empowered you?* *Do you feel you have the same opportunities as the Foursquare founder?*	Equality Trained Inclusion Empower Opportunities	The same upward mobility that male counterparts experience is not an option for females. There has been very little experience of a support system in the past for women within the denomination (although the denomination is making more recent efforts to provide this since Connection 2022). The current executive team *desires* to empower women yet seems bound. Men that could empower women do not. Men empower men.	"I was given a significant church with adequate resources." "I was included and [i.e., but] told I was there as a token." "A woman made way for me at the decision-making table." "Women *should* feel safe spiritually and physically." "I was fired for attending a prayer meeting while being a Foursquare employee, and no one intervened."	Token No encouragement No development Excluded Spiritually abused Lack of exposure Opportunities Inclusion Nepotism Systemic patriarchy Injustice The affiliation has hurt my family.

Table 12. Personal Responses

Questions (14-15)	Key Concepts	Main Points	Elaboration	Key Words Used
To what extent is your gender limiting your call? To what extent are you likely to recommend other female senior leaders seeking denominational affiliation to The Foursquare Church?	Limiting Recommendation to women to champion and support other women by including them and putting their names forward for opportunities.	Men do not know how to train women. Poor theology is being taught. Christian history is not being properly examined. The limitations women experience are as much due to their own theological misunderstanding of women's roles as they are due to men limiting them. I would absolutely encourage other women to pursue an affiliation with the church.	"Men need to be educated on how [to be inclusive with women] and [how to] train [and support] women, and on *why* women are equal." "If healthy theology is not taught, it is not surprising that women are unsure of their place." "Women are visualizing other women in lead roles." "We don't have it all right as a denomination, but at least women have some representation in The Foursquare Church." "I would not encourage my daughters to go into the ministry."	Exclusion Too corporate I can't say, "Yes." The organization is not healthy. Too many spiritual abuse stories. What is the common denominator? Women are not being developed and released.

Data collected from the interview process proved critical to this project. However, significant information was shared during the interviews that is outside this project's scope.

Conclusion

This study aimed to explore the underrepresentation of female senior leaders within The Foursquare Church, with a target population of senior female leaders recruited from a pool of 132 eligible subjects in the United States. The participants' average years of service to The Foursquare Church was fifteen. The research design involved two platforms for gathering data—a survey with questions divided into four categories, to provide a foundation for interview questions. The length of the interviews ranged between sixty and ninety minutes. The interviews were transcribed and coded, allowing the research. The two data-gathering instruments, the survey and the interview, allowed me to gain insight from the perceptions, opinions, and experiences of the participants.

Chapter 9 focuses on the summary of the research project by individual segments. The Foursquare Church in the early years, today, and in the future is observed alongside the results of the qualitative research findings. I also suggest future studies concerning gender inequity within The Foursquare Church.

Chapter 9

Summary and Recommendations

Introduction

This chapter presents a summary of the study and conclusions drawn from the data presented in the previous chapters. The two questions this project seeks to answer are Why are women underrepresented at the senior leadership level within The Foursquare Church? and Are there commonalities between the participants' experiences considering the decline? This chapter also provides a summary of the biblical-theological and literature reviews. Finally, it concludes with recommendations for further research.

Summary of Biblical-Theological Review

Select Scholarship of Intentional Inclusion of Women in Lead Roles

The fulcrum for Part Two is the debate concerning the authority and biblical right of women to hold leadership roles within the church. The review reveals that throughout the Bible, women have been placed in leadership. In the beginning, God created males and females to be equal, then sin entered and created a hierarchy, which is evident in patriarchy. Yet, the biblical texts reveal numerous women in leadership.

Female leaders in the Old Testament, include judges, prophetesses, and warriors. For example, Deborah, the first female judge of Israel

(Judg. 4:4-5:31), leads the people into victory and provides rest to the land. The prophecy of Huldah (2 Kgs. 22:15-20; 2 Chron. 34:22-33) ignites a revival in which Israel repents, destroys the altars to foreign gods, and removes idolatry from the land.

> In the New Testament, women were church planters, theologians, leaders, and advancers of the Kingdom.

In the New Testament, women were church planters, theologians, leaders, and advancers of the Kingdom. Junia was the first and only woman to be called an apostle. Priscilla was a prominent leader, businesswoman, and theologian. The fourth-century church father, Chrysostom, known for making statements against women, said, "Priscilla took Apollos, an eloquent man and mighty in the Scriptures, but knowing only the baptism of John; and she instructed him in the way of the Lord and made him a teacher brought to completion (Acts 18:24-25)."[1]

Challenging New Testament Passages Concerning Women in Leadership Roles

Throughout Scripture are stories of women fulfilling the roles of ministry leadership: i.e., pastors, teachers, evangelists, apostles, and prophets. Despite these biblical accounts, male scholars continue to

---

[1] Catherine Clark Kroeger, "John Chrysostom's First Homily on the Greeting to Priscilla and Aquilla," CBE International, July 30, 1991, acccssed July 12, 2022, https://www.cbeinternational.org/resource/article/priscilla-papers-academic-journal/john-chrysostoms-first-homily-greeting-priscilla. See also John Chrysostom, "Homily 40 on the Acts of the Apostles," New Advent, accessed January 5, 2023, https://www.newadvent.org/fathers/210140.htm.

interpret Scripture with biases as women struggle for positions within the church. First Timothy 2:12 is the most commonly misused and misinterpreted passage used against women and their leadership although female teachers and leaders can be found throughout Scripture. Women exercising spiritual authority over men in a male-dominated context (Junia and Huldah) can also be witnessed in Scripture. When the Holy Spirit's power was released at Pentecost, it was indiscriminately given, and the global Church was launched with the absence of gender barriers, just as Joel prophesied (see Joel 2:26-28).

When the Holy Spirit's power was released at Pentecost, it was indiscriminately given, and the global Church was launched with the absence of gender barriers, just as Joel prophesied (see Joel 2:26-28).

Finally, women can be found prophesying, teaching, and having spiritual authority throughout Scripture rather than remaining silent. The evidence affirms that the Pauline injunctions about women are specific to situations in the churches to which he is referencing versus a global mandate.

Jesus's Response to Women

Jesus ministered to women, He allowed women to minister to Him, and to become disciples (in a society in which a Rabbi's followers were only males). Jesus treats men and women equally and with respect and compassion. Jesus rejected Jewish cultural principles concerning women's menstrual cycle, causing her to be defiled and excluding her from the synagogue, periodic feasts, and various functions of faith.

Jesus taught where women were required to stay, the women's court. When teaching in the Temple, Jesus chose the outer court to allow women to hear His message. With intentionality, He made sure the women heard His teaching. He included them in discipleship training in preparation for ministry. Women attended His birth, death, and burial.

Jesus taught where women were required to stay, the women's court.

Deborah Gill and Barbara Cavaness share this reminder of Jesus's egalitarian style of teaching by noting,

> Jesus balanced the parables with male and female activities so that both genders would receive the message. For example, He compared the kingdom of God to a mustard seed which a man planted and then to the years that a woman mixed in her dough (Luke 13:19-21). When teaching about lost sinners, Jesus used first a male shepherd who loses a sheep and then a woman who loses a coin as examples (Luke 15:3-10). He matched the parable of the persistent widow with the parable of the Pharisee and the tax collector to teach about justice (Luke 18:1-14). And He used both the story of the ten virgins and the story of the three servants to teach about the kingdom of heaven (Matt 25:1-30).[2]

Complementarians claim that men and women are created equal yet hold designated roles. On the contrary, Jesus sees men and women

---

[2] Deborah M. Gill and Barbara Cavaness, *God's Women Then and Now* (Springfield, MO: Grace and Truth, 2004), 75.

created in God's image and gifted equally, placing no restrictions upon their roles within the church.[3]

Significant Aspects of the Literature Review

The Foursquare Church—Early Years

The Foursquare Church was founded in Los Angeles in 1923 by Aimee Semple McPherson. Within months of establishing the institution, McPherson opened a Bible college (LIFE) to train men and women for ministry. From the beginning the women students outnumbered the men students; a fact that is still evident (in 2022, LIFE reports 250 male students and 351 females).[4] Although McPherson never joined a feminist movement, she sought to prepare women to be leaders, preachers, and teachers of the gospel.

Although McPherson never joined a feminist movement, she sought to prepare women to be leaders, preachers, and teachers of the gospel.

Female leaders can be found planting, leading, and serving throughout the denomination's history. The keystones of The Foursquare Church stipulate that women are to be a part of leadership, which includes a positional statement affirming women

---

[3] Gretchen E. Ziegenhals, "Women in Ministry: Beyond the Impasse," Baylor University Center for Christian Ethics, 2009, accessed July 13, 2022, https://baylor.edu/content/services/document.php/98766.pdf.

[4] "Institutional Data and Disclosures," Life Pacific University, January 1, 2022, https://lifepacific.edu/about/institutional-data-and-disclosures/.

at all levels of leadership and the necessity for ongoing efforts to train and equip women is evident within the institution.[5]

The Foursquare Church—Today

According to a 2016 Barna study of female representation in several denominations, The Foursquare Church is lowest with only 9 percent.[6] Table 13 below contains a summary of this Barna study.

Table 13. Female Statistical Representation

Year	Denomination	Representation
2022	The Foursquare Church	9 percent
2022	AG	28 percent
2020	UMC	32 percent
2019	PC(USA)	38 percent
2017	Episcopal Church	33 percent

Although women are often affirmed from the pulpit, the pathway to leadership is anything but straight. Women report discrimination, exclusion, hurdles, hindrances, and struggles in their attempt to obey the call of God on their lives. Examples of obstacles include preaching against women in leadership, an active Boys' Club culture, and the Billy Graham Rule.

> Although women are often affirmed from the pulpit, the pathway to leadership is anything but straight.

Women in ministry leadership report similar experiences as women in the political, corporate, and academic sectors. Yet, statistics

---

[5] Sam Rockwell, ed., *Identity Keystones: What Makes Us Foursquare* (Los Angeles, CA: The Foursquare Church, 2017).

[6] David Kinnaman, "What Americans Think about Women in Power," Barna Group, March 8, 2017, accessed August 3, 2022, https://www.barna.com/research/americans-think-women-power.

indicate that those in the secular workplace enjoy a greater acceptance from society in their roles than women in the religious sector. Nevertheless, power struggles of various kinds remain among women pursuing leadership positions.

The Foursquare Church—The Future

The response by the church to the question, what is a woman's place in the church? should be inclusivity. As The Foursquare Church focuses on increasing females as senior leaders, it can strengthen its commitment to live out God's original purpose for the institution by considering the following aspects of prophetic vision articulated in Part Two of this project.

1. **God-Ordained**—Aimee Semple McPherson as the steward of The Foursquare Church. This appointment affirms that God intended for women to be released and empowered within this institution. Rather than credentialed women representing 9 percent of female leaders, 50 percent or greater should be the goal. Rather than 7 percent of senior female leaders, 50 percent or greater of women holding these key roles should be the target.

2. **Females Championing Other Female Leaders**— Women can and must use their influence to become allies for other women. Women understand the bias, the injustice, the inclusion, and the political messiness of climbing uphill.

3. **Male Leaders Being Other-Focused**—Foursquare men must discard any position in conflict to the equal standing of males and females. Men must recognize that exclusion

diminishes God in people's eyes, but inclusiveness weakens patriarchy.[7]

4. **God-Approved**—In order to be approved, an evaluation must take place. Statistically, women hold more associate, bachelor, master, and doctorate degrees than men.[8] For equality, inclusion, and mutuality to be the goal within The Foursquare Church, an egalitarian-belief organization, education should play the same role as it did at the institution's beginning. Concerning what *should* be, imagine the institution's accountability to license those holding a professional degree, M.Div., from an appropriately accredited egalitarian seminary, prior to planting, leading, or holding office within The Foursquare Church. This intentionality would give women, statistically more educated, the same opportunity as men. Those pastors grandfathered could work through a ten-year timeframe to obtain the academic requirements.

Inclusivity within The Foursquare Church senior leadership can increase as the denomination takes such steps.

Summary of the Research Results

The participant research reveals the following about The Foursquare Church: An institution that promotes egalitarianism in its policy is not always evident in the actions of the institution. Inequality, injustice, discrimination, and exclusion result from patriarchy. Resources for leadership development and mentoring for women is

---

[7] Linda Romey, "It's time to Find out Where Religious Life Can Go without Patriarchy," Global Sisters Report, January 18, 2022, https:www/globalsistersreport.org/news/religious-life/column/its-time-find-out-where-religious-life-can-go-without-patriarchy.

[8] National Center for Education Statistics, "Fast Facts: Degrees Conferred by Race/Ethnicity and Sex (2018-1019)," accessed August 31, 2022, https://nces/ed/gov/fastfacts/display.asp?id=72.

deficient. Despite the number of educated and experienced women in the queue for leadership there is a lack of opportunity for leadership roles. Lack of education concerning women is damaging to gender parity.

Lack of education concerning women is damaging to gender parity.

In a denomination founded by a woman, there is a gap in training women for leadership roles. There is some hope as the current executive leadership team is intentionally placing more women in decision-making roles.

Recommendations for The Foursquare Church

To address gender inequity within The Foursquare Church, the results of this project offer the following recommendations:

1. An educational requirement of an M.Div. from an approved egalitarian-believing seminary prior to planting, leading, or serving at the senior level. The education requirement will allow women, statistically having more education than men, to have the same opportunity as men within the institution.

2. Raise the percentage of female district supervisors to 50 percent. This increase would provide an opportunity to recommend to the Board of Directors individuals for pastoral appointments.

3. Encourage cross-gender mentoring and create programs to support these relationships.

4. Support educational efforts with funding through scholarships.

5. Address reports of injustice, discrimination, and sexism promptly.

6. Create opportunities to hear from female senior leaders within the institution about their experiences, setting a goal of having at least 50 percent of female licensed minsters scrving as lead pastors.

7. Do not remain neutral. Be an advocate for women in ministry in general and for equal representation and opportunity of women in leadership roles within the denomination.

Recommendations for Future Study

The focus of this study is gender parity within The Foursquare Church. As the denomination reports, 9 percent of females in The Foursquare Church serve in senior leadership positions.[9] Only five participants were part of this study, therefore, a further study with more women is recommended as is a study on the impact of male versus female district supervisors. Additionally, a comparative study of the various Foursquare Presidents to evaluate the number of female leaders appointed during each of their terms would provide additional statistical data.

---

[9] "This is Foursquare: Cabinet Report 2022," 3.

Appendix A

Survey

Female Perceptions on Diverse Leadership in The Foursquare Church

Please choose one answer for each of the following fifteen questions.

1. What is your title in your current (current/previous)?
    o Senior or Lead Pastor
    o Co-senior or co-lead pastor (with my spouse)
    o Co-senior or co-lead pastor (with a male counterpart)
    o Co-senior or co-lead pastor (with another woman)
    o Other

2. How long did/have you served in the above-mentioned leadership role?
    o 0 to 5 years
    o More than 5 years but less than 10 years
    o More than 10 but less than 15 years
    o More than 15 years

3. Marital Status during the above referenced leadership assignment?
    o Single
    o Married
    o Divorced
    o Widowed

4. Did you have children during the above referenced leadership period?
    - o Yes
    - o No

5. Which of the following describe your primary duty in your church?
    - o Preaching
    - o Teaching Bible Studies
    - o Women ministry leader
    - o Children or youth ministry leader
    - o Pastoral Counselor
    - o Missions Pastor
    - o Other

6. To what extent have you felt affirmed within the district where you serve The Foursquare Church
    - o Not at all
    - o Very little
    - o Somewhat
    - o To a good extent
    - o To a great extent

7. To what extent have you felt affirmed among your peers within The Foursquare Church?
    - o Not at all
    - o Very little
    - o Somewhat
    - o To a good extent
    - o To a great extent

8. To what extent have you felt affirmed from the national level of The Foursquare Church?
    - o Not at all
    - o Very little
    - o Somewhat
    - o To a good extent
    - o To a great extent

9. To what extent have you experienced upward mobility/advancement in ministry as your male counterparts?
    - o Not at all
    - o Very little
    - o Somewhat
    - o To a good extent
    - o To a great extent

10. To what extent has Foursquare met your expectations as a support system to aid in leadership growth through coaching?
    - o Not at all
    - o Very little
    - o Somewhat
    - o To a good extent
    - o To a great extent

11. As a female senior leader, at what extent do you feel in the *community* of The Foursquare Church?
    - o Not at all
    - o Very little
    - o Somewhat
    - o To a good extent
    - o To a great extent

12. To what extent do you feel that Foursquare empowers women in key roles within the denomination?
    - o Not at all
    - o Very little
    - o Somewhat
    - o To a good extent
    - o To a great extent

13. To what extent do you agree that opportunities to preach, to lead, and to hold executive office in the denomination given to Foursquare founder, Aimee Semple McPherson, are available to you?
    - o Not at all
    - o Very little
    - o Somewhat
    - o To a good extent
    - o To a great extent

14. To what extent do you feel your gender is limiting your call in The Foursquare Church?
    - o Not at all
    - o Very little
    - o Somewhat
    - o To a good extent
    - o To a great extent

15. To what extent are you likely to recommend the Foursquare denomination to other female senior leaders seeking denominational affiliation and ministry leadership opportunities?
    - o Not at all
    - o Very little
    - o Somewhat
    - o To a good extent
    - o To a great extent

Appendix B

Participant Interview Responses

Participant A

1. "Theologically speaking, The Foursquare Church is inherently complementarian and not egalitarian."

2. "The women are more of a problem than you realize. Many are still wrestling with their theology concerning women and their roles based on what has been poured into them (fathers, other male figures, etc.)."

3. I asked, "What did Rolf McPherson bring to The Foursquare Church following the death of Aimee Semple McPherson, his mother and founder?" She said, "It is the classic story of appointing someone with a similar anointing. He had an administrative anointing rather than a ministerial anointing, which was very limited. So The Foursquare Church transitioned from being spirit led to administratively led."

4. Discrimination within The Foursquare Church has been an issue for some time. She said, "President Harold Helm, in 1998, stood up in Tulsa, Oklahoma and repented on behalf of Foursquare for their behavior towards women and the exclusion of women in leadership roles."

5. "In the 40s, women were exiled to missions only. The church grabbed hold of the model that a good wife stayed home and cared for the children and the home. Foursquare embraced this model also. It was a racist move." Participant A quoted

another leader: "Women are allowed to lead black men in Africa, the poor man in India, those in a third world country, but not lead the white man in America." "Women responded to Foursquare's exclusion by creating a movement called United Foursquare Women because they were taken away from the pulpits and excluded in church planting." This decision was okay with Foursquare because the women were in the field ministering." She pointed out this behavior as systemic racism within The Foursquare Church. "Most larger organizations that have women and are not sure what to do with them send them to the mission field."

6. "Women were licensed and ordained under Aimee, but under Rolf's leadership, they gave token licenses to women. If the man was licensed, they automatically licensed the wife."

7. "Very few women are appointed in The Foursquare Church to churches of significant size. So women have to plant churches and grow them from the ground up rather than wait for a male leader to sponsor or recommend them in a place of a healthy church. We have not until we appoint a woman to a church of significant size and resources."

8. "People have a theological basis they are unaware of."

9. "There is bullying in our denomination." "In past leadership, specific leaders have been guilty of wanting everyone to be happy and get along rather than confronting the problems within our denomination."

10. "Patriarchy began, in my opinion, with Rolf McPherson."

11. "Our denomination has no lack of female leaders. The women are trained and developed just as are the men. However, our men need training concerning women and their place within the denomination."

12. "There are significant leaders within our denomination that chauvinistic and function as high-level complementarians, at best."

13. "The patriarchal problem exists in pockets within our movement. However, I do not believe patriarchy exists at a high level within the denomination because we have a good balance of male and female representation in the boardroom."

14. "I do not feel we have a glass ceiling in our denomination; we have a glass floor. The problem is not corporate. The problem is not in our bylaws or our governance. Our problem is not our willingness to appoint a woman to a specific role. It is on the ground floor. People do not know how to raise leaders, in general."

15. "I have been a token within our denomination. The leaders were intentional, and I saw it as an opportunity for women. Some women recognize tokenism and are offended by it. I see it as an opportunity to dialogue at the table."

16. "Women feel they are not invited to the table. Men also feel uninvited, unheard, or given opportunities like others."

17. "I think one of the greatest problems Foursquare has moving forward is determining what to do with the co-pastor model when the woman is the senior leader yet they both feel called."

18. "We might be low in our numbers concerning women, but we are not zero."

Participant B

1. "I had one female role model and one male supporter. From the beginning, they encouraged me to move forward."

2. "I only saw women preaching in the pulpit a couple of times, if ever. There were no female leaders in the church where I

attended in the preacher/teacher role. Licensed women were unique and served in a support role."

3.   "One of the problems in The Foursquare Church is that no one is intentionally developing female leaders. There are programs available for mentoring, but for a woman that has never seen a female pastor or even sat under the teaching of a female in the pulpit, they have no confidence they should move forward in a coaching/mentoring relationship."

4.   "The potential to lead and the call of God on a person's life are not the same thing. However, I feel there is a blind spot in our licensing process, and women are licensed because they are women and have the potential to be a leader rather than because they are called. I also do not believe that when men were being licensed early on, they were asked about their theology concerning female pastors. That is part of the problem in our denomination. It was assumed that since a woman founded the denomination, they were affirming women in lead roles. Now, they are backtracking to try and repair the problem. Now, they ask new licensees and refuse a license if they disagree with the egalitarian stand in The Foursquare Church."

5.   Men are not developing women; they are developing men. They do not have the skill set to train, support, and release women. The men in The Foursquare Church need to be educated in this area. Part of the problem is the BGR."

6.   Participant B said, "Women in The Foursquare Church are not even sure women can hold every role within The Foursquare Church."

7.   When asked about Patriarchy in The Foursquare Church, she responded, "Things changed when Rolf McPherson took office."

8. "We must do better in appointing, licensing, and accountability."

9. She mentioned the abuse/harassment/hiding it under the rug cases plaguing The Foursquare Church. She said, "Repentance equals change of direction. Although there appears to be deep repentance concerning the stories that came out at Connection, these stories cannot be ignored. Something other than "I am sorry for what happened" is necessary. Admit wrong. Admit neglect. Then, there should be fruit following words."

10. "Women should feel safe spiritually and physically within our churches. What are the common denominators of abuse within our denomination?"

11. "If you say I am valuable and influential, let me be."

Participant C

1. "There are a lot of well-prepared women in Foursquare Church."

2. "The oldest issue within the denomination is generational patriarchy."

3. "God is raising up women, but I do not feel that patriarchy will be changed from the inside out."

4. "There is no lack of training for women within The Foursquare Church. They are being trained better and more than ever."

5. "Men do not know how to train women."

6. "Aimee Semple McPherson was silenced and controlled nearing the end of her ministry by Giles McKnight. Her children had to ask permission to visit her. I believe this controlling relationship had an impact upon the denomination

and quite possibly upon her son. Rolf is known for being controlling."

7. "The Foursquare Church claims "middle of the road" as one of their keystones. Yet, in order to be "in the middle of the road," you must know where the boundaries are on either side."

Participant D

1. "I do not look to the denomination for affirmation."

2. "Do not give your heart to an organization. Give your heart to people."

3. "The denomination is no more than a legal covering and that…is all."

4. "I have received tools from individuals but none from the institution."

5. "You will be disposed of eventually, within the denomination."

6. "Rolf came into the denomination and was conservative, controlling, and heavy-handed. The denomination was older white men in charge."

7. "Annually, I pay $195.00 to keep my license current and basically receive nothing for it."

Participant E

1. "Nepotism is alive and well in the denomination."

2. "Rolf McPherson brought a spirit of control in the denomination."

3. "There is no real encouragement for women."

4. "Pastor's wives are recognized more than are female pastors."

5. "Oh, so you are the token women," is a statement I have heard many times.

6. "Victims of spiritual abuse experience the same type of trauma as a rape victim. We should take it as seriously as we do rape."

7. "Lots of women that have left the denomination are actively involved in ministry through a 501©3."

8. "I am not related to anyone within the denomination so I don't get the same opportunities are others might."

9. "The denomination does not respect the education that women have."

10. "Women plant churches because they are not likely to be appointed into a healthy one."

11. "The face of the church has to change. We are no longer making disciples."

12. "People that really have a heart for God, don't question women's role."

Appendix C

Survey Results in Graph Format[1]

Q1 What is your title in your church (current/previous)

Answered: 5   Skipped: 0

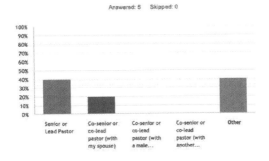

ANSWER CHOICES	RESPONSES	
Senior or Lead Pastor	40.00%	2
Co-senior or co-lead pastor (with my spouse)	20.00%	1
Co-senior or co-lead pastor (with a male counterpart)	0.00%	0
Co-senior or co-lead pastor (with another woman)	0.00%	0
Other	40.00%	2
TOTAL		5

---

[1] Title of project at the time of survey administration was "The Perceptions of Women on Diversity and Leadership in The Foursquare Church." Prior to project completion the title was changed to "Female Perceptions on Diverse Leadership in The Foursquare Church."

Q2 How long did/have you served in the above-mentioned leadership role?

Answered: 5   Skipped: 0

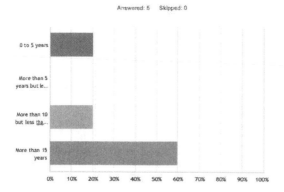

ANSWER CHOICES	RESPONSES	
0 to 5 years	20.00%	1
More than 5 years but less than 10 years	0.00%	0
More than 10 but less than 15 years	20.00%	1
More than 15 years	60.00%	3
TOTAL		5

Q3 Marital Status during the above referenced leadership assignment?

Answered: 5   Skipped: 0

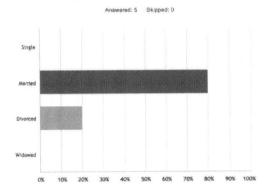

ANSWER CHOICES	RESPONSES	
Single	0.00%	0
Married	80.00%	4
Divorced	20.00%	1
Widowed	0.00%	0
TOTAL		5

Diverse Leadership in The Foursquare Church

Q4 Did you have children during the above referenced leadership period?

Answered: 5   Skipped: 0

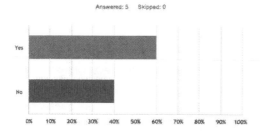

ANSWER CHOICES	RESPONSES	
Yes	60.00%	3
No	40.00%	2
TOTAL		5

Q5 Which of the following describe your primary duty in your church?

Answered: 5   Skipped: 0

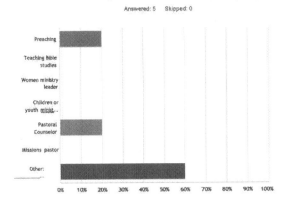

ANSWER CHOICES	RESPONSES	
Preaching	20.00%	1
Teaching Bible studies	0.00%	0
Women ministry leader	0.00%	0
Children or youth ministry leader	0.00%	0
Pastoral Counselor	20.00%	1
Missions pastor	0.00%	0
Other:	60.00%	3
TOTAL		5

Q6 To what extent have you felt affirmed within the district where you serve the Foursquare Church?

Answered: 5   Skipped: 0

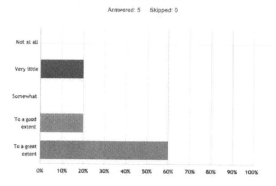

ANSWER CHOICES	RESPONSES	
Not at all	0.00%	0
Very little	20.00%	1
Somewhat	0.00%	0
To a good extent	20.00%	1
To a great extent	60.00%	3
TOTAL		5

Q7 To what extent have you felt affirmed among your peers within the Foursquare Church?

Answered: 5   Skipped: 0

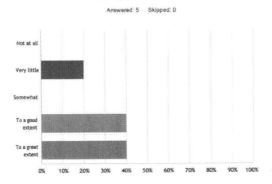

ANSWER CHOICES	RESPONSES	
Not at all	0.00%	0
Very little	20.00%	1
Somewhat	0.00%	0
To a good extent	40.00%	2
To a great extent	40.00%	2
TOTAL		5

Q8 To what extent have you felt affirmed from the national level of the Foursquare Church?

Answered: 5   Skipped: 8

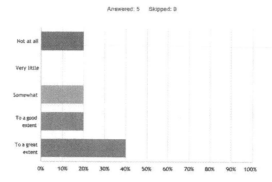

ANSWER CHOICES	RESPONSES	
Not at all	20.00%	1
Very little	0.00%	0
Somewhat	20.00%	1
To a good extent	20.00%	1
To a great extent	40.00%	2
TOTAL		5

Q9 To what extent have you experienced upward mobility/advancement in ministry as your male counterparts?

Answered: 5   Skipped: 0

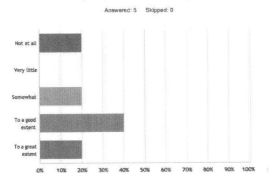

ANSWER CHOICES	RESPONSES	
Not at all	20.00%	1
Very little	0.00%	0
Somewhat	20.00%	1
To a good extent	40.00%	2
To a great extent	20.00%	1
TOTAL		5

167

Q10 To what extent has Foursquare met your expectations as a support system to aid in leadership growth through coaching?

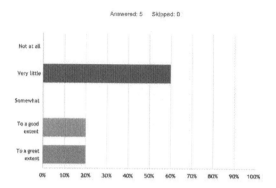

Answered: 5   Skipped: 0

ANSWER CHOICES	RESPONSES	
Not at all	0.00%	0
Very little	60.00%	3
Somewhat	0.00%	0
To a good extent	20.00%	1
To a great extent	20.00%	1
TOTAL		5

Q11 As a female senior leader, at what extent do you feel included in the community of the Foursquare Church?

Answered: 5   Skipped: 0

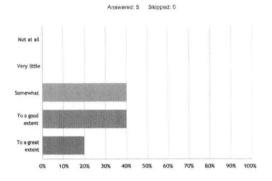

ANSWER CHOICES	RESPONSES	
Not at all	0.00%	0
Very little	0.00%	0
Somewhat	40.00%	2
To a good extent	40.00%	2
To a great extent	20.00%	1
Total Respondents: 5		

169

Q12 To what extent do you feel that Foursquare empowers women in key roles within its denomination?

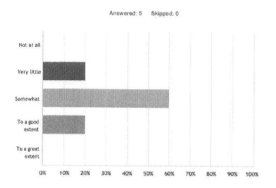

Answered: 5   Skipped: 0

ANSWER CHOICES	RESPONSES	
Not at all	0.00%	0
Very little	20.00%	1
Somewhat	60.00%	3
To a good extent	20.00%	1
To a great extent	0.00%	0
TOTAL		5

Diverse Leadership in The Foursquare Church

The Perceptions of Women on Diversity and Leadership in The Foursquare   SurveyMonkey
Church

Q13 To what extent do you agree that opportunities to preach, to lead, and to hold executive office in the denomination given to Foursquare founder, Aimee Semple McPherson, are available to you?

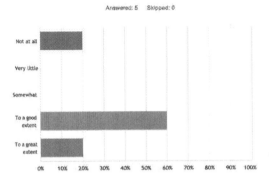

Answered: 5   Skipped: 0

ANSWER CHOICES	RESPONSES	
Not at all	20.00%	1
Very little	0.00%	0
Somewhat	0.00%	0
To a good extent	60.00%	3
To a great extent	20.00%	1
TOTAL		5

171

Q14 To what extent do you feel your gender is limiting your call in the Foursquare Church?

Answered: 5   Skipped: 0

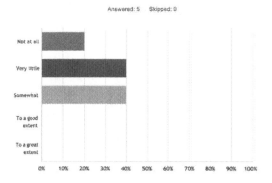

ANSWER CHOICES	RESPONSES	
Not at all	20.00%	1
Very little	40.00%	2
Somewhat	40.00%	2
To a good extent	0.00%	0
To a great extent	0.00%	0
TOTAL		5

Q15 To what extent are you likely to recommend the Foursquare denomination to other female senior leaders seeking denominational affiliation and ministry leadership opportunities?

Answered: 5   Skipped: 0

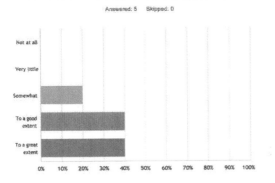

ANSWER CHOICES	RESPONSES	
Not at all	0.00%	0
Very little	0.00%	0
Somewhat	20.00%	1
To a good extent	40.00%	2
To a great extent	40.00%	2
TOTAL		5

173

Glossary

The Billy Graham Rule (BGR) is for men in the organization and requires them to avoid being alone with the opposite gender in any context, whether in pastoral counseling, discipleship, meeting, eating, or ministry travel, to prevent false accusations or gossip that could taint a minister's reputation. The original intent was to keep traveling ministers from the potential of scandal, financial abuse, or sexual immorality.[1]

Complementarianism is a theological view that men are uniquely qualified and called to do the work of the ministry at the highest levels of leadership. Women can hold secondary leadership positions if their teachings are limited to children and other women. Male and females are considered equal yet have different roles.

Credentialed refers to the official qualifications or documentation necessary to minister. The Foursquare Church has two facets in credentialing: licensing and ordination. A minister is eligible for ordination consideration following two years of faithful ministerial service in The Foursquare Church.

Egalitarianism is a theological view that both men and women are equally called and equipped by God to do the work of the ministry at all leadership levels.

The International Church of The Foursquare Gospel is a religious body incorporated as the formal organization sometimes referred to

---

[1] Billy Graham, "What's the Billy Graham Rule'?," *Billy Graham Evangelistic Association,* last modified July 23, 2019, accessed July 02, 2022, https://billygraham.org/story/the-modesto-a-declaration-of-biblical-integrity.

herein as "The Foursquare Church." However, in 2012, the global Foursquare community recognized distinctives held common as a denomination and as a movement (Article 3.2 in Bylaws). The six distinctives include the following: (1) kingdom partnerships, (2) sound doctrine, (3) empowering leadership, (4) family relationships, (5) Spirit empowerment, and (6) shared mission.2 The Foursquare Church is a Pentecostal denomination founded by Aimee Semple McPherson in 1927. The Foursquare gospel, which is that Jesus is the Savior, Baptizer with the Holy Spirit, Healer, and Soon Coming King has been preached worldwide.

Patriarchy refers to a "social organization marked by the supremacy of the father in the clan or family, the legal dependence of wives and children, and the reckoning of descent and inheritance in the male line ... broadly [the term refers to the] control by men of a disproportionately large share of power. ... a society or institution organized according to the principles or practices of patriarchy."3

---

2 "The Foursquare Global Distinctives," Foursquare.org, accessed January 5, 2023, https://www.foursquare.org/about/beliefs/#global-distinctives.
3 "Patriarchy," Merriam-Webster Dictionary, accessed January 2, 2023, https://www.merriam-webster.com/dictionary/patriarchy.

Select Resources

Alexander, Kimberly Ervin, and James P. Bowers. *What Women Want: Pentecostal Women Ministers Speak for Themselves.* Eugene: Wipf & Stock, 2018.

Archer, Melissa. "Women in Ministry: A Pentecostal Reading of New Testament Texts." In *Women in Pentecostal and Charismatic Ministry: Informing a Dialogue on Gender, Church, and Ministry,* edited by Margaret English de Alminana and Lois E. Olena, 35-56. Vol. 21 of Global Pentecostal and Charismatic Studies. Leiden: Brill, 2017.

Barr, Beth Allison. *The Making of Biblical Womanhood.* Grand Rapids, MI: Brazos Press, 2021.

Campbell-Reed, Eileen. "No Joke: Resisting the Culture of Disbelief." Eileen Campbell-Reed. May 9, 2020. Accessed August 3, 2022. https://cdn.eileencampbellreed.org/wp-content/uploads/No_Joke_Campbell-Reed_Rev_4-25-2018_Submitted_Version.pdf.

Chaves, Mark. *Ordaining Women: Culture and Conflict in Religious Organizations.* Cambridge, MA: Harvard University Press, 1999.

———. *Why Are There (Still!) So Few Women Clergy?* Faith and Leadership. Accessed September 19, 2022. https://faithandleadership.com/markchaves-why-are-there-still-so-few-women-clergy.

Clark-Soles, James. *Interpretation Resource for the Use of Scripture in the Church: Women in the Bible.* Louisville: Westminster John Knox Press, 2020.

Cunningham, Carolyn M. *Gender, Communication, and the Leadership Gap. Women and Leadership: Research, Theory, and Practice.* Charlotte, NC: Information Age Publishing, 2017.

Duran, Saehee H. "Intentional Male Allies/Advocates: How Male Leaders Can Successfully Champion Female Ministers in the Assemblies of God U.S.A." D.Min. proj., Southeastern University, Lakeland, FL, 2022. FireScholars. Accessed April 13, 2022. https://firescholars.seu.edu/dmin/23/.

Epp, Eldon Jay. *Junia: The First Woman Apostle.* Minneapolis, MN: Fortress, 2005.

Elting, Liz. "How to Navigate a Boy's Club Culture." Forbes Magazine. July 30, 2018. August 3, 2022. https://www.forbes.com/sites/lizelting/2018/07/27/how-to-navigate-a-boys-club-culture/?sh=516aba74025c.

Fee, Gordon D. "The Priority of Spirit Gifting for Church Ministry." In *Discovering Biblical Equality: Complementarity without Hierarchy,* edited by Ronald W. Pierce, Rebecca Merrill Groothuis, and Gordon D. Fee, 241-54. Leicester: IVP Academic, 2005.

Finlay, Barbara. "Do Men and Women Have Different Goals for Ministry? Evidence from Seminarians." *Sociology of Religion* 57, no. 3 (Fall, 1996): 311-18, https://www.proquest.com/scholarly-journals/do-men-women-have-different-goals-ministry/docview/216769739/se-2?accountid=40702. http://www.jstor.org/stable/3712159.

Gill, Deborah M., and Barbara Cavaness. *God's Women Then and Now.* Springfield, MO: Grace and Truth, 2004.

Haddad, Mimi R. "Examples of Women's Leadership in the Old Testament and Church History." In *Women in Pentecostal and Charismatic Ministry: Informing A Dialogue on Gender, Church, and Ministry*, edited by Margaret English de Alminana and Lois E. Olena, 59-69. Leiden: Brill, 2017.

Keener, Craig S. "Interpretations and Applications of 1 Corinthians 14:34-35." Marg Mowczko, April 21, 2022. Accessed July 12, 2022. https://margmowczko.com/interpretations-applications-1-cor-14_34-35.

———. *Paul, Women & Wives: Marriage and Women's Ministry in the Letters of Paul.* Peabody, MA: Hendrickson, 2004.

Matthews, Heather. "Uncovering and Dismantling Barriers for Women Pastors." CBE International. February 3, 2022. Accessed May 16, 2022. https://www.cbeinternational.org/resource/article/priscilla-papers-academic-journal/uncovering-and-dismantling-barriers-women.

McKnight, Scot. *The Blue Parakeet: Rethinking How You Read the Bible.* 2nd ed. Grand Rapids, MI: Zondervan, 2018.

Mead, Patrick. "Who 'Killed' Junia? Part One." The Junia Project. April 30, 2014. Accessed July 15, 2022. https://juniaproject.com/who-killed-junia-part-one/.

———. "Who 'Killed' Junia? Part Two." The Junia Project. May 2, 2014. Accessed July 15, 2022. https://juniaproject.com/who-killed-junia-part-two/.

Payne, Leah. *Gender and Pentecostal Revivalism: Making a Female Ministry in the Early Twentieth Century.* New York: Palgrave MacMillan, 2015.

Payne, Philip Barton, and Vince Huffaker. *Why Can't Women Do That?: Breaking down the Reasons Churches Put Men in Charge.* Boulder, CO: Vinati Press, 2021.

"Prominent Biblical Scholars on Women in Ministry." Marg Mowczko. January 25, 2022. June 2, 2022. https://margmowczko.com/prominent-biblical-scholars-on-women-in-ministry.

Qualls, Joy E. A. *God Forgive Us for Being Women: Rhetoric, Theology, and the Pentecostal Truth.* Eugene, OR: Pickwick Publications, 2018.

Stephenson, Lisa P. *Dismantling the Dualisms for American Pentecostal Women in Ministry: A Feminist-Pneumatological Approach.* Vol. 9 of Global Pentecostal and Charismatic Studies. Leiden: Brill, 2012.

———. "Credentialed Women in the Foursquare Church: An Exploration of Opportunities and Hindrances in Leadership" PhD diss., Fuller Theological Seminary, 2013.

Williams, Terran. *How God Sees Women: The End of Patriarchy.* Cape Town South Africa: The Spiritual Bakery Publications, 2022.

Witherington, Ben. "Why Arguments Against Women in Ministry Aren't Biblical." Patheos. June 2, 2015. Accessed July 12, 2022. https://www.patheos.com/blogs/bibleandculture/2015/06/02/why-arguments-against-women-in-ministry-arent-biblical/.

Ziegenhals, Gretchen E. "Women in Ministry: Beyond the Impasse." Baylor University Center for Christian Ethics. 2009. Accessed July 13, 2022. https://www.baylor.edu/content/services/document.php/98766.pdf.

Bibliography

"6 Ways That Women Can Champion Each Other at Work." Lean In. Accessed August 16, 2022. https://leanin.org/tips/workplace-ally#!

Abbasianchavari, Arezou, and Alexandra Moritz. "The Impact of Role Models on Entrepreneurial Intentions and Behavior: A Review of the Literature." *Management Review Quarterly* 71 (2021): 1-40. https://link.springer.com/article/10.1007/s11301-019-00179-0.

"About Us." The Foursquare Church. Accessed September 19, 2019. https://www.foursquare.org/about.

Adams, Jim. "Introduction." In *Women in Ministry Leadership: A Summary of the Biblical Position of the Foursquare Church Concerning God's Grace and a Woman's Potential under His Sovereignty and Call.* Rev. ed., edited by Steve Schell, 11. Los Angeles: Foursquare Media, 2021.

———. "Position Statements." In *Women in Ministry Leadership: A Summary of the Biblical Position of the Foursquare Church Concerning God's Grace and a Woman's Potential under His Sovereignty and Call.* Rev. ed., edited by Steve Schell, 7-10. Los Angeles: Foursquare Media, 2021.

Adams, Jim J., Jack W. Hayford, John A. Mazariegos, and Jim Scott. *Women in Ministry Leadership Ministry: A Summary of the Biblical Position of the Foursquare Church Concerning God's Grace and a Women's Potential Under His Sovereignty and Call.* Los Angeles, CA: Foursquare Media, 2007.

Adams, Jim, Wanda Brackett, Daniel Brown, John Mazariegos, Doretha O'Quinn, Susan Rowe, Steve Schell, and Jim Scott. *Women in Ministry Leadership: A Summary of the Biblical Position of the Foursquare Church Concerning God's Grace and a Woman's Potential under His Sovereignty and Call.* Los Angeles: Foursquare Media, 2021.

Alaqahtani, T. H. "The Status of Women in Leadership." Research Gate. Accessed July 6, 2022. https://www.researchgate.net/profile/Tahani-Alqahtani-2/publication/340514638_The_Status_of_Women_in_Leadership/links/60580b44458515e8345ff7bd/The-Status-of-Women-in-Leadership.pdf.

Alexander, Kimberly Ervin, and James P. Bowers. *What Women Want: Pentecostal Women Ministers Speak for Themselves.* Eugene: Wipf & Stock, 2018.

Alter, Robert. *The Hebrew Bible: A Translation with Commentary.* Vol. 2. New York New York: W.W. Norton & Company, 2019.

"Americans See Catholic Clergy Sex Abuse as an Ongoing Problem." Pew Research Center's Religion & Public Life Project. Pew Research Center. May 30, 2020. Accessed August 31, 2022. https://www.pewresearch.org/religion/2019/06/11/americans-see-catholic-clergy-sex-abuse-as-an-ongoing-problem/.

"Angelus Temple Gives Aid to Thousands of Needy: Free Dining Has Also Been Opened." *The Florence Times*, March 18, 1932, 2.

Anila, K. P., and V. Krishnaveni. "Influence of Family Environment and Work Environment on Work Life Balance among Women Employees." *International Journal of Management Research and Reviews* 6, no. 3 (March 2016): 341-47, https://www.proquest.com/scholarly-journals/influence-family-environment-work-on-life-balance/docview/1786453047/se-2?accountid=40702.

Archer, Melissa. "Women in Ministry: A Pentecostal Reading of New Testament Texts." In *Women in Pentecostal and Charismatic Ministry: Informing a Dialogue on Gender, Church, and Ministry*, edited by Margaret English de Alminana and Lois E. Olena, 35-56. Vol. 21 of Global Pentecostal and Charismatic Studies. Leiden: Brill, 2017.

Ashley, Jacqueline. "Council Post: Why Multidimensional Self-Care Is Essential to Better Leadership." Forbes Magazine. June 28, 2021. Accessed August 31, 2022. https://www.forbes.com/sites/forbescoachescouncil/2021/06/28/why-multidimensional-self-care-is-essential-to-better-leadership/?sh=73fe830d5d56.

Assemblies of God. "Statistics on the Assemblies of God (USA): Female Ministers 1977 through 2021." Accessed August 10, 2022. http://www.ag.org/About/Statistics.

Auld, A. G. Joshua. *Judges, Ruth: The Daily Study Bible Series*. Philadelphia: Westminster, 1984.

"BDAG 378." CBE International. Accessed June 25, 2022. https://www.cbeinternational.org/.

Barr, Beth Allison. *The Making of Biblical Womanhood*. Grand Rapids, MI: Brazos Press, 2021.

Barrett, C. K. *Acts 15-28*. Vol. 2 of *International Critical Commentary*. T & T Clark, London: T & T Clark, 1998.

Bartram, Sharon. "What Is Wrong with Current Approaches to Management Development in Relation to Women in Management Roles?" *Women in Management Review* 20, issue 2 (March 1, 2005). Emerald Insight. Accessed August 3, 2022. https://www.emerald.com/insight/content/doi/10.1108/09649420510584445/full/html.

Bassler, Jouette M. "1 Cor 12:3: Curse and Confession in Context." *Journal of Biblical Literature* 101, no. 3 (1982): 415-18. https://doi.org/10.2307/3260353.

Baumann, Heide. "Stories of Women at the Top: Narratives and Counternarratives of Women's (Non-) Representation in Executive Leadership." *Palgrave Communications* 3, no. 1 (December 2017): 1-13. https://www.proquest.com/scholarly-journals/stories-women-at-top-narratives-counternarratives/docview/2282435661/se-2?accountid=40702.

Belleville, Linda, Segovis, Schoon, Dick, Nacusi, Leibson, Billadeau, et al. "Ἰουνιαν ... Ἐπισημοι Ἐν Τοις Ἀποστολοις: A Re-Examination of Romans 16.7 in Light of Primary Source Materials." BELLEVILLE, LINDA | download, 2005. https://ur.booksc.me/book/38987095/500e1b.

"Beliefs." Foursquare. Accessed August 2, 2022.
  https://www.Foursquare.org/about/beliefs/.

Bennett, Judith M. *History Matters: Patriarchy and the Challenge of Feminism.*
  Philadelphia, PA: University of Pennsylvania Press, 2007.

Bernardi, Richard A., Susan M. Bosco, and Veronica L. Columb. "Does Female
  Representation on Boards of Directors Associate with the 'Most Ethical
  Companies' List?" ResearchGate, September 2009. *Corporate Reputation Review*
  12, no. 3 (2009): 270-80. https://www.researchgate.net/profile/Susan-
  Bosco/publication/228173088_Does_Female_Representation_on_Boards_o
  f_Directors_Associate_with_the_'Most_Ethical_Companies'_List/links/55b
  f7c5408aed621de139660/Does-Female-Representation-on-Boards-of-
  Directors-Associate-with-the-Most-Ethical-Companies-List.pdf.

Bethune, Magaela C. "2020 Geographical Trends of Gender Disparities in
  Composition and Compensation for UMC Clergy." Resource UMC.
  Accessed August 10, 2022,
  https://www.resourceumc.org/en/partners/gcsrw/home/content/2020-
  geographic-trends-of-gender-disparities-in-composition-and-compensation-
  for-umc-clergy.

Bickle, Vanessa. "No Longer Male and Female: Why Do We Still Separate by
  Gender in Church?" CBE International. January 19, 2022. Accessed June 5,
  2022. https://www.cbeinternational.org/resource/article/mutuality-blog-
  magazine/no-longer-male-and-female-why-do-we-still-separate-gender.

Block, Daniel Isaac. *Judges, Ruth.* Vol. 6 of *The New American Commentary.* Nashville:
  Broadman & Holman Publishers, 1999.

Blomberg, Craig L. *Matthew: An Exegetical and Theological Exposition of Holy Scripture.*
  Book 22 of *The New American Commentary (NAC).* Gen. ed. David S. Dockery.
  Nashville, TN: Broadman Press, 1992.

Bonine, Maria, Charlotte Eversoll, Michelle E. Knight, Michael Szydlowski, and
  Kelly Ylitalo. 2020. "In the Image of God: Facing Differences." *Currents in
  Theology and Mission* 47 (2): 27-29.
  https://search.ebscohost.com/login.aspx?direct=true&db=lsdar&AN=ATL
  AiFZK200430001081&site=ehost-live.

Borchert, Gerald. *John 1-11.* Vol. 25A of *New American Commentary.* Nashville:
  Broadman & Holman, 2002.

Borowski, Amanda. "The Building of Angelus Temple." News | Resources,
  October 8, 2020. Accessed August 31, 2022.
  https://resources.foursquare.org/the_building_of_angelus_temple/.

Bradley, Sheri. "This is a Question of Culture, Power, and Value, Not Role." CBE
  International. July 7, 2022. Accessed July 13, 2022.
  https://www.cbeinternational.org/resource/
  article/mutuality-blog-magazine/question-culture-power-and-value-not-role.

Brescoll, Victoria L. "Leading with Their Hearts? How Gender Stereotypes of
  Emotion Lead to Biased Evaluations of Female Leaders." *The Leadership
  Quarterly* 27, issue 3 (June 2016): 415-28.
  http://www.sciencedirect.com/science/article/pii/S1048984316000151.

Brooten, Bernadette. "'Junia … Outstanding among the Apostles' (Romans 16:7)
  (1)." Women Priests, June 29, 2021. Accessed July 15, 2022.
  https://womenpriests.org/articles-books/brooten-junia-outstanding-among-
  the-apostles-romans-167-1.

Brown, Genevieve. *Women Leaders: Advancing Careers. Research on Women and Education.* Charlotte, NC: Information Age Publishing, 2011.

Bruce, F. F. "Women in the Church: A Biblical Survey." *Christian Brethren Review* 33 (1982): 7-14. Theological Studies. Accessed June 2, 2022. https://theologicalstudies.org.uk/pdf/cbr/women_bruce.pdf.

———. *Paul: Apostle of the Heart Set Free.* Grand Rapids, MI: Eerdmans, 1981.

———. *The Epistles to the Colossians, to Philemon, and to the Ephesians.* Grand Rapids, MI: Eerdmans, 1984.

Buck, Pearl S. *Of Men and Women: How to Be for Each Other.* New York: Open Road Integrated Media, 2017.

Buckalew, Erik, Alexis Konstantinopoulos, Jonathan Russell, and Seif El-Sherbini. "The Future of Female CEOs and their Glass Ceiling." *Journal of Business Studies Quarterly* 3, no. 4 (June 2012): 145-53. https://www.proquest.com/scholarly-journals/future-female-ceos-their-glass-ceiling/docview/1036929638/se-2?accountid=40702.

Bushnell, Horace. "Women's Suffrage: The Reform Against Nature: Bushnell, Horace, 1802-1876: Free Download, Borrow, and Streaming Bushnell." Internet Archive. New York: Scribner, January 1, 1869. https://archive.org/details/womenssuffragere00bushrich.

Business Bliss Consultants FZE. "Gender Gap in Leadership: Barriers and Challenges for Women." UKDiss.com. 2018. Accessed August 31, 2022. https://ukdiss.com/examples/gender-gap-in-leadership.php.

Butcher, Andy. "Life Pacific University Appoints Angie Richey as President." News + Resources, August 1, 2019. https://resources.foursquare.org/life-pacific-university-appoints-angie-richey-as-president/.

Butler, Trent, ed. *Judges.* Word Biblical Commentary 8. Nashville, TN: Thomas Nelson, 2009.

Campbell-Reed, Eileen. "No Joke: Resisting the Culture of Disbelief." Eileen Campbell-Reed. May 9, 2020. Accessed August 3, 2022. https://cdn.eileencampbellreed.org/wp-content/uploads/No_Joke_Campbell-Reed_Rev_4-25-2018_Submitted_Version.pdf.

Cavanaugh, Lynn Varacalli. "The Power of the Male Ally: Engaging Men, Advancing Women." Progressive Women's Leadership. October 21, 2016. Accessed August 31, 2022. https://www.progressivewomensleadership.com/the-power-of-the-male-ally-engaging-men-advancing-women/.

Center for Women and Business at Bentley University. "Men as Allies: Engaging Men to Advance Women in the Workplace." Bentley University, Spring 2017. Accessed August 31, 2022. https://wit.abcd.harvard.edu/files/wit/files/cwb_men_as_allies_research_report_spring_2017.pdf.

Chaves, Mark. *Ordaining Women: Culture and Conflict in Religious Organizations.* Cambridge, MA: Harvard University Press, 1999.

———. *Why Are There (Still!) So Few Women Clergy?* Faith and Leadership. Accessed September 19, 2022. https://faithandleadership.com/markchaves-why-are-there-still-so-few-women-clergy.

Chrysostom, John. "Homily 40 on the Acts of the Apostles." New Advent. Accessed January 5, 2023. https://www.newadvent.org/fathers/210140.htm.

Clark-Soles, James. *Interpretation Resource for the Use of Scripture in the Church: Women in the Bible*. Louisville: Westminster John Knox Press, 2020.

Collins, John J., and Daniel C. Harlow. *The Eerdmans Dictionary of Early Judaism*. Grand Rapids, MI: William B. Eerdmans, 2010.

Cook, Alison, and Christy Glass. "Women and Top Leadership Positions: Towards an Institutional Analysis." March 21, 2013. Wiley Online Library. Accessed August 31, 2022. https://onlinelibrary.wiley.com/doi/abs/10.1111/gwao.12018.

Coppins, Wayne. "Peter Arzt-Grabner on the Interpretation of IOYNIAN in Rom 16.7 (Paulus Handbuch Series)." German for Neutestamentler. March 16, 2016. Accessed July 13, 2022. https://germanforneutestamentler.com/2014/06/23/paulus-handbuch-peter-arzt-grabner-on-the-interpretation-of-%CE%B9%CE%BF%CF%85%CE%BD%CE%B9%CE%B1%CE%BD-in-rom-16-7/.

Craft, Carolyn M. *Women Pastors*. *Cross Currents* 46, no. 1 (Spring, 1996): 133, https://www.proquest.com/scholarly-journals/women-pastors/docview/214950869/se-2?accountid=40702.

Creswell, John W., and Cheryl N. Poth, *Qualitative Inquiry & Research Design: Choosing among Five Approaches*. 4th ed. Los Angeles, CA: SAGE, 2018.

Cunningham, Carolyn M. *Gender, Communication, and the Leadership Gap. Women and Leadership: Research, Theory, and Practice*. Charlotte, NC: Information Age Publishing, 2017.

"Current Numbers." Center for American Women and Politics. Accessed July 4, 2022. https://cawp.rutgers.edu/facts/current-numbers.

"Declaration of Faith Compiled by Aimee Semple McPherson." Foursquare. Accessed January 5, 2023. https://foursquare-org.s3.amazonaws.com/assets/Declaration_of_Faith.pdf.

Dennis, Michal Robert, and Adrianne Dennis Kunkel. "Perceptions of Men, Women, and CEOs: The Effects of Gender Identity." *Social Behavior & Personality: An International Journal* 32, no. 2 (2004): 155-71. Doi:10.22224/sbp.2004.32.2.155.

Dewalt, Samantha L. "Gender Equality and Authenticity: A Study of Women in IT Leadership." EdD diss., Pepperdine University, Malibu, CA, 2017. https://digitalcommons.pepperdine.edu/etd/771/.

Dillard, Raymond B., and Tremper Longman, III. *An Introduction to the Old Testament*. Grand Rapids, MI: Zondervan, 1994.

Dixon, Rob. "Raising up Allies: A Standardized Pathway for Developing Men into Allies to Women." CBE International, July 31, 2020. Accessed August 31, 2022. https://www.cbeinternational.org/resource/article/priscilla-papers-academic-journal/raising-allies-standardized-pathway-developing.

Duran, Saehee H. "Intentional Male Allies/Advocates: How Male Leaders Can Successfully Champion Female Ministers in the Assemblies of God U.S.A." D.Min. proj., Southeastern University, Lakeland, FL, 2022. FireScholars. Accessed April 13, 2022. https://firescholars.seu.edu/dmin/23/.

Dwyer, Bonnie. "Gerry Chudleigh Explains the History of Headship Theology." Spectrum Magazine. May 2, 2014. Accessed July 12, 2022. https://spectrummagazine.org/article/bonnie-dwyer/2014/05/02/gerry-chudleigh-explains-history-headship-theology.

Eagly, Alice, and Linda Carli. "Women and the Labyrinth of Leadership." Harvard Business Review. September 1, 2007. Accessed August 3, 2022. https://hbr.org/2007/09/women-and-the-labyrinth-of-leadership.

Edwards, Korie L. "Role Strain Theory and Understanding the Role of Head Clergy of Racially Diverse Churches." *Sociology of Religion* 75, no. 1 (2014): 57-79. https://doi.org/10.1093/socrel/srt047.

Epp, Eldon Jay. *Junia: The First Woman Apostle.* Minneapolis, MN: Fortress, 2005.

Ekine, Adefunke O. "Women in Academic Arena: Struggles, Strategies and Personal Choices." *Gender Issues* 35, no. 4 (December 2018): 318-29. Accessed August 31, 2022. https://www.proquest.com/scholarly-journals/women-academic-arena-struggles-strategies/docview/2044607018/se-2?accountid=40702.

Elmuti, Dean, Heather Jia, and Henry H. Davis. "Challenges Women Face in Leadership Positions and Organizational Effectiveness: An Investigation." *Journal of Leadership Education* 8, issue 2 (2009). Accessed August 31, 2022. https://journalofleadershiped.org/jole_articles/challenges-women-face-in-leadership-positions-and-organizational-effectiveness-an-investigation/.

Elting, Liz. "How to Navigate a Boy's Club Culture." Forbes Magazine. July 30, 2018. August 3, 2022. https://www.forbes.com/sites/lizelting/2018/07/27/how-to-navigate-a-boys-club-culture/?sh=516aba74025c.

"Engaging Men in Gender Initiatives: What Change Agents Need to Know (Report)." Catalyst, May 4, 2009. Accessed August 31, 2022. https://www.catalyst.org/research/engaging-men-in-gender-initiatives-what-change-agents-need-to-know/.

Epstein, Cynthia Fuchs. "Great Divides: The Cultural, Cognitive, and Social Bases of the Global Subordination of Women." *American Sociological Review* 72, no. 1 (February 2007): 1-22. https://www.proquest.com/scholarly-journals/great-divides-cultural-cognitive-social-bases/docview/218846104/se-2?accountid=40702.

"Executive Power: An Overview." Legal Information Institute. Legal Information Institute. Accessed July 22, 2022. https://www.law.cornell.edu/wex/executive_power.

"Fact Sheet: Health Disparities and Stress." American Psychological Association. American Psychological Association, 2012. Accessed August 31, 2022. https://www.apa.org/topics/racism-bias-discrimination/health-disparities-stress.

Fausset, Andrew Robert, A. R. Fausset, and David Brown. *Jeremiah–Malachi.* Vol. IV of *A Commentary, Critical, Experimental, and Practical, on the Old and New Testaments.* Logos Bible Software. Accessed August 21, 2022. https://www.logos.com/product/169281/a-commentary-critical-experimental-and-practical-on-the-old-and-new-testaments-vol-iv-jeremiah-malachi.

Fee, Gordon D. "The Priority of Spirit Gifting for Church Ministry." In *Discovering Biblical Equality: Complementarity without Hierarchy,* edited by Ronald W. Pierce, Rebecca Merrill Groothuis, and Gordon D. Fee, 241-54. Leicester: IVP Academic, 2005.

———. *The First Epistle to the Corinthians.* Grand Rapids, MI: Eerdmans Publishing Company, 1987.

Finlay, Barbara. "Do Men and Women Have Different Goals for Ministry?
Evidence from Seminarians." *Sociology of Religion* 57, no. 3 (Fall, 1996): 311-18,
https://www.proquest.com/scholarly-journals/do-men-women-have-
different-goals-ministry/docview/216769739/se-2?accountid=40702.
http://www.jstor.org/stable/3712159.

"Foursquare Church." News + Resources, October 27, 2020.
https://www.foursquare.org/resources.

"The Foursquare Global Distinctives," Foursquare.org, accessed January 5, 2023,
https://www.foursquare.org/about/beliefs/#global-distinctives.

"Foursquarecabinetreport-2022-Final - Amazon Web Services." Accessed August
31, 2022. https://foursquare-leader.s3.us-east-
1.amazonaws.com/about_us/business/2022-Cabinet-Report.pdf.

"Foursquare Missions International." Foursquare Missions International.
Accessed May 25, 2022. https://www.foursquaremissions.org.

"Foursquare Ministry Training." Foursquare Leader. Accessed April 1, 2022.
https://foursquare-
leader.s3.amazonaws.com/education/Institutes_Handbook.pdf.

Freedman, R. David. "Woman, a Power Equal to Man." The BAS Library.
November 5, 2015. Accessed July 12, 2022.
https://www.baslibrary.org/biblical-archaeology-review/9/1/6.

Friesen, Aaron. *Foursquare Identity Keystones.* Los Angeles: Foursquare Media, 2018.

Funk, Cary, and Kim Parker. "Women and Men in STEM Often at Odds over
Workplace Equity." Pew Research Center's Social & Demographic Trends
Project. Pew Research Center. August 21, 2020. Accessed August 31, 2022.
https://www.pewresearch.org/social-trends/2018/01/09/women-and-men-
in-stem-often-at-odds-over-workplace-equity/.

Garland, David E. *1 Corinthians.* Grand Rapids, MI: Baker Academic, 2003.

"Gender and Leadership in the PC(USA)." Presbyterian Mission Agency. Summer
2016. Accessed August 3, 2022.
https://www.presbyterianmission.org/resource/gender-leadership-pcusa/.

Gill, Deborah M., and Barbara Cavaness. *God's Women Then and Now.* Springfield,
MO: Grace and Truth, 2004.

Graf, Nikki. "Sexual Harassment at Work in the Era of #Metoo." Pew Research
Center's Social & Demographic Trends Project. April 4, 2018. Accessed
August 3, 2022. https://www.pewresearch.org/social-
trends/2018/04/04/sexual-harassment-at-work-in-the-era-of-metoo.

Graham, Billy. "What's 'the Billy Graham Rule'?" Billy Graham Evangelistic
Association. July 23, 2019. August 3, 2022.
https://billygraham.org/story/the-modesto-manifesto-a-declaration-of-
biblical-integrity/.

Grenz, Stanley J. *Theology for the Community of God.* Grand Rapids, MI: Eerdmans
Publishing Company, 1994.

Groothius, Rebecca Merrill. *Good News for Women: A Biblical Picture of Gender
Equality.* Grand Rapids, MI: Baker Books, 1997.

———. *Women Caught in the Conflict: The Culture War between Traditionalism and
Feminism.* Eugene, OR: WIPF & Stock Publishers, 1997.

Haddad, Mimi R. "Examples of Women's Leadership in the Old Testament and
Church History." In *Women in Pentecostal and Charismatic Ministry: Informing A*

Dialogue on Gender, Church, and Ministry, edited by Margaret English de Alminana and Lois E. Olena, 59-69. Leiden: Brill, 2017.

———. "International Women's Day and CBE." CBE International. March 10, 2022. Accessed August 31, 2022. https://www.cbeinternational.org/resource/article/mutuality-blog-magazine/international-womens-day-and-cbe.

Hall, Christopher Alan. *Learning Theology with the Church Fathers*. Downers Grove, IL: InterVarsity Press, 2002.

Harding, Lori. "Complementarianism Exists in Egalitarian Organizations and Churches Because of Patriarchy." CBE International. June 15, 2022. Accessed June 7, 2022. https://www.cbeinternational.org/resource/article/mutuality-blog-magazine/complementarianism-exists-egalitarian-organizations-and.

"Harvard Women in Tech + Allies." Harvard Women in Tech + Allies, 2017. Accessed August 31, 2022. https://wit.abcd.harvard.edu/.

Hassey, Janette. *No Time for Silence: Evangelical Women in Public Ministry around the Turn of the Century*. Grand Rapids, MI: Academic Books, 1986.

Hayford, Jack. "The Pentecostal Pilgrimage and the Emerging Church." Second Annual Pentecostal Leaders Series. The Wilson Institute for Pentecostal Studies." Costa Mesa, CA, February 17, 2011.

———. *Women in Leadership Ministry*. Edited by Steve Schell. Los Angeles: Foursquare Media, 2007.

Henry, Matthew. *Matthew Henry's Commentary on the Whole Bible: Complete and Unabridged in One Volume*. Peabody, MA: Hendrickson, 1994.

Hestenes, Roberta. "Scripture and the Ministry of Women." *Theology, News & Notes*. (December 1978): 9.

Hill, Catherine, Kevin Miller, Kathleen Benson, and Grace Handley. "Barriers and Bias: The Status of Women in Leadership." American Association of University Women. Accessed August 3, 2022. https://ww3.aauw.org/research/barriers-and-bias/ February 29, 2016. https://eric.ed.gov/?id=ED585546.

Hinchliffe, Emma. "The Number of Female CEOs in the Fortune 500 Hits an All-Time Record." Fortune, October 29, 2020. Accessed August 31, 2022. https://fortune.com/2020/05/18/women-ceos-fortune-500-2020/.

Hinchliffe, Emma. "Roz Brewer, Thasunda Brown Duckett, Karen Lynch Make up Record Number of Female Fortune 500 CEOS." Fortune. May 23, 2022. Accessed August 3, 2022. https://fortune.com/2022/05/23/female-ceos-fortune-500-2022-women-record-high-karen-lynch-sarah-nash.

"A Historic Look at the Seventh Day Adventist Church." Seventh-day Adventist Church. Accessed August 8, 2022. https://www.adventist.org/who-are-seventh-day-adventists/history-of-seventh-day-adventists/.

"History." The Foursquare Church. May 30, 2022. Accessed August 2, 2022. https://www.foursquare.org/about/history.

"History and Heritage." Life Pacific College. Accessed January 5, 2023. https://lifepacific.edu/about/history-heritage/.

Homan, Patricia, and Amy Burdette. "When Religion Hurts: Structural Sexism and Health in Religious Congregations." *American Sociological Review* 86, issue 2 (2021): 234-55. https://doi.org/10.1177/0003122421996686. Podcast interview with Jaimee Panzarella. April 2021. Scribd. Accessed August 12,

2022. https://www.scribd.com/podcast/501326895/American-Sociological-Review-When-Religion-Hurts-Structural-Sexism-and-Health-in-Religious-Congregations-Authors-Patricia-Homan-and-Amy-Burdette-d.

Houltberg, Loren. "Cultivating Key Practices for Resilience in Pastoral Ministry among United States Foursquare Pastors." D.Min. proj., Fuller Seminary School of Theology, 2020 https://digitalcommons.fuller.edu/dmin/408.

House, Paul. *1, 2 Kings*. Vol. 8 of *The New American Commentary*. Nashville: Broadman & Holman, 1995.

Hoyt, Michael A. and Cara L. Kennedy. "Leadership and Adolescent Girls: A Qualitative Study of Leadership Development." *American Journal of Community Psychology* 42, no. 3-4 (December 2008): 203-19. https://www.proquest.com/scholarly-journals/leadership-adolescent-girls-qualitative-study/docview/205344715/se-2?accountid=40702.

Hull, Gretchen Gaebelein. *Equal to Serve: Women and Men in the Church and Home.* Old Tappan, NJ: Fleming H. Revell, 1987.

Hymowitz, Carol, and Timothy D. Schellhard. "The Glass Ceiling: Why Women Can't Seem to Break the Invisible Barrier That Blocks Them from the Top Jobs." *Wall Street Journal*, March 24, 1986.

"Institutional Data and Disclosures." Life Pacific University, January 1, 2022. https://lifepacific.edu/about/institutional-data-and-disclosures/.

International Church of the Foursquare Gospel. "Corporate Bylaws 2019 Edition." Foursquare Leader. Accessed July 4, 2022. https://foursquare-leader.s3.us-east-1.amazonaws.com/about_us/business/Bylaws_English.pdf.

"Introducing the Foursquare Church." The Foursquare Church. Accessed July 9, 2022. http://foursquare-org.s3.amazonaws.com/resources/Print_Brochure_Introducing_Foursquare_Church_English_bw.pdf.

Inyamah, Deborah C. "Contrasting Perspectives on the Role of the Feminine in Ministry and Leadership Roles in John 4 and 1 Timothy 2:11-15." *Journal of Religious Thought* 60-63, no. 1-2 (2008): 87-IV, https://www.proquest.com/scholarly-journals/contrasting-perspectives-on-role-feminine/docview/1313216066/se-2?accountid=40702.

Irving, Justin A., and Mark L. Strauss. *Leadership in Christian Perspective: Biblical Foundations and Contemporary Practices for Servant Leaders.* Grand Rapids, MI: Baker Academic a division of Baker Publishing Group, 2019.

Jamieson, Robert, A. R. Fausset, and David Brown. *A Commentary, Critical and Explanatory on the Whole Bible: with Introduction to Old Testament Literature, a Pronouncing Dictionary of Scripture Proper Names, Tables of Weights and Measures, and an Index to the Entire Bible.* Grand Rapids, MI: Eerdmans, 1935.

———. *The Old Testament: From Song of Solomon to Malachi.* Vol. 2 of *Commentary Critical and Explanatory on The Whole Bible.* Oak Harbor: Logos Research Systems, Inc., 1997.

Javadian, Golshan, and Robert P. Singh. "Examining Successful Iranian Women Entrepreneurs: An Exploratory Study." *Gender in Management* 27, no. 3 (2012): 148-64. https://www.proquest.com/scholarly-journals/examining-successful-iranian-women-entrepreneurs/docview/1010038554/se-2?accountid=40702.

Jewett, Paul King *Man as Male and Female.* Grand Rapids: MI: Eerdmans Publishing, 1975.

————. *Ordination of Women: An Essay on the Office of Christian Ministry*. Eugene, OR: Wipf & Stock Publishers, 2012.

Johns, Loretta, and Janice Watson. "Leadership Development of Women Preparing for Ministry." *Journal of Research on Christian Education* 15, no. 2 (Fall, 2006): 111-42, https://www.proquest.com/scholarly-journals/leadership-development-women-preparing-ministry/docview/594820091/se-2?accountid=40702.

Johnson, Alan F., ed. *How I Changed My Mind about Women in Leadership: Compelling Stories from Prominent Evangelicals*. Grand Rapids, MI: Zondervan, 2010.

Johnson, Brad, and David Smith. "How Men Can Become Better Allies to Women." *Harvard Business Review*. August 15, 2019. Accessed August 31, 2022. https://hbr.org/2018/10/how-men-can-become-better-allies-to-women.

Kärkkäinen, Veli-Matti. *Christology: A Global Introduction*. Grand Rapids, MI: Baker Academic, 2003.

————. *The Doctrine of God: A Global Introduction*. Grand Rapids, MI: Baker Academic, 2004.

Karpowitz, Christopher F., Tali Mendelberg, and Lee Shaker. "Gender Inequality in Deliberative Participation." Cambridge Core (Cambridge University Press). August 9, 2012. Accessed August 31, 2022. https://www.cambridge.org/core/journals/american-political-science-review/article/gender-inequality-in-deliberative-participation/CE7441632EB3B0BD21CC5045C7E1AF76.

Kawakami, Christine, Judith B. White, and Ellen J. Langer. "Mindful and Masculine: Freeing Women Leaders from the Constraints of Gender Roles." *Journal of Social Issues* 56, no. 1 (2000): 49-63. Citeseerx. Accessed August 31, 2022. https://citeseerx.ist.psu.edu/viewdoc/download?doi=10.1.1.1065.1308&rep=rep1&type=pdf.

Keener, Craig S. "Interpretations and Applications of 1 Corinthians 14:34-35." Marg Mowczko, April 21, 2022. Accessed July 12, 2022. https://margmowczko.com/interpretations-applications-1-cor-14_34-35.

————. *Paul, Women & Wives: Marriage and Women's Ministry in the Letters of Paul*. Peabody, MA: Hendrickson, 2004.

Keil, Carl Friedrich, and Franz Delitzsch. *Joshua, Judges, Ruth, 1 & 2 Samuel*. Vol. 2 of *Commentary on the Old Testament*. Peabody, MA: Hendrickson, 1996.

Kessler, Martina. "Female Leaders in the 21st Century in a Masculine World/Vroulike Leiers in Die 21ste Eeu in 'n Manlike Wêreld." *Koers* 79, no. 2 (2014): 1-7. https://www.proquest.com/scholarly-journals/female-leaders-21st-century-masculine-world/docview/1752156809/se-2?accountid=40702.

King, Michelle. "KPMG's Lynne Doughtie on Why Women Are the Future of Work." Forbes Magazine, May 23, 2017. Accessed August 31, 2022. http://www.forbes.com/sites/michelleking/2017/05/23/kpmgs-lynne-doughtie-on-why-women-are-the-future-of-work/#129291f8114c.

Kinnaman, David. "38% of U.S. Pastors Have Thought about Quitting Full-Time Ministry in the Past Year." Barna Group, November 16, 2021. https://www.barna.com/research/pastors-well-being/.

———. "State of the Church." Barna Group, 2020.
https://www.barna.com/research/state-of-the-church.

———. "What Americans Think about Women in Power." Barna Group, March 8, 2017. Accessed August 3, 2022.
https://www.barna.com/research/americans-think-women-power.

Kostenberger, Andreas J. *John.* Baker Exegetical Commentary on the New Testament. Grand Rapids, MI: Baker Academic, 2004.

Kramer, Jillian. "Here's What's Keeping Women from the C-Suite." Glamour. October 1, 2015. Accessed August 31, 2022.
https://www.glamour.com/story/women-barriers-ceo.

Krause, Susan Faye. "Leadership: Underrepresentation of Women in Higher Education." PhD diss., University of New England, January 2017.
https://www.une.edu/sites/default/files/leadership_underrepresentation_of_women_in_higher_education.pdf.

Kreuzer, Barbara Katherine. "Women and Leadership: The Effect of Gender, Gender-Role Orientation, Socioeconomic Status, and Parental Influence on Women's Aspirations to Leader Roles." EdD diss., Western Michigan University, 1992.
https://scholarworks.wmich.edu/cgi/viewcontent.cgi?article=2965&context=dissertations&httpsredir=1&referer=.

Kroeger, Catherine Clark. "John Chrysostom's First Homily on the Greeting to Priscilla and Aquila." CBE International. July 30, 1991. Accessed July 12, 2022. https://www.cbeinternational.org/resource/article/priscilla-papers-academic-journal/john-chrysostoms-first-homily-greeting-priscilla.

Kroeger, Richard Clark, and Catherine Clark Kroeger. *Suffer Not a Woman: Rethinking 1 Timothy 2:11-15 in Light of Ancient Evidence.* Grand Rapids, MI: Baker Books, 1992.

Lange, John Peter et al., *A Commentary on the Holy Scriptures: Judges* Bellingham, WA: Logos Research Systems, 2008.

LaRosa, Judith H. "Executive Women and Health: Perceptions and Practices." *American Journal of Public Health* 80 (December 1990): 1450-54.
https://ajph.aphapublications.org/doi/epdf/10.2105/AJPH.80.12.1450.

Lamsa, Anna-Maija, and Teppo Sintonen. "A Discursive Approach to Understanding Women Leaders in Working Life: JBE." *Journal of Business Ethics* 34, no. 3 (December 2001): 255-67.
https://www.proquest.com/scholarly-journals/discursive-approach-understnading-women-leaders/docview/198106341/se-2?accountid=40702.

LeGrand, Sara, Rae Jean Proeschold-Bell, John James, and Amanda Wallace. "Healthy Leaders: Multilevel Health Promotion Considerations for Diverse United Methodist Church Pastors." *Journal of Community Psychology* 41, no. 3 (April 2013): 303-321. Accessed July 6, 2022.
https://www.researchgate.net/publication/235852305_Healthy_Leaders_Multilevel_Health_Promotion_Considerations_For_Diverse_United_Methodist_Church_Pastors.

Leslie, W. H. "The Concept of Woman in the Pauline Corpus in Light of the Social and Religious Environment of the First Centry." Ph.D. diss., Northwestern University, 1976.

Lincoln, Andrew T. *Ephesians.* Word Biblical Commentary 42. Nashville, TN: Thomas Nelson, 1990.

Lindars, Barnabas. *Deborah's Song: Women in the Old Testament.* Manchester: J. Rylands University Library of Manchester, 1983.

Lofgren, Jenn. "Council Post: How to Be a Champion for Women in Leadership." Forbes Magazine, March 11, 2019. Accessed August 31, 2022.

Lummis, Adair T. "Women with a Mission: Religion, Gender and the Politics of Women Clergy." *Sociology of Religion* 67, no. 3 (Fall, 2006): 338-9, https://www.proquest.com/scholarly-journals/women-with-mission-religion-gender-politics/docview/216753310/se-2?accountid=40702.

Lummis, Adair T., and Paula D. Nesbitt. "Women Clergy Research and the Sociology of Religion." OUP Academic. Oxford University Press, December 1, 2000. https://academic.oup.com/socrel/article-abstract/61/4/443/1642945.

Lyola, Thomas. "A Template for the Future: Resonant Leadership in The Song of Deborah." *Journal of International Women's Studies* 22, Issue 6 (June 2021): 3-10.

Marchetti, Christine. "Ordained Women in the Church." Priscilla Papers, 2021. Accessed July 13, 2022. https://www.cbeinternational.org/resource/article/priscilla-papers-academic-journal/ordained-women-church

"Marjorie Matthews." (1916-1986): The First Woman Elected a Bishop in the United Methodist Church—1980." The United Methodist Church (General Commission on Archives and History). Accessed July 9, 2022. http://www.gcah.org/history/biographies/marjorie-matthews.

Martin, D. Michael. *1, 2 Thessalonians.* Vol. 33 of *New American Commentary.* Nashville, TN: Broadman & Holman Publishers, 1995.

Marutzky, Regg. "The Bible and Gender: Roles, Leadership, and Ministry (1 Cor 14:33-40)." Biblia, March 20, 2020. Accessed July 12, 2022. https://biblia.com/bible/esv/1-corinthians/14/33-40.

Masci, David. "The Divide over Ordaining Women." Pew Research Center. Accessed May 30, 2020. https://www.pewresearch.org/fact-tank/2014/09/09/the-divide-over-ordaining-women.

Mathis, Rick. "Disciple-Making in Foursquare Missioning." *QUADRUM: Journal of the Foursquare Scholars Fellowship* 1, no. 2 (November 2018), 178-211.

Mathisen, Gro Ellen, Torvald Ogaard, and Einar Marnburg. "Women in the Boardroom: How Do Female Directors of Corporate Boards Perceive Boardroom Dynamics?" *Journal of Business Ethics* 116, no. 1 (August 2013): 87-97. https://www.proquest.com/scholarly-journals/women-boardroom-how-do-female-directors-corporate/docview/1433066751/se-2?accountid=40702.

Matthews, Heather. "Uncovering and Dismantling Barriers for Women Pastors." CBE International. February 3, 2022. Accessed May 16, 2022. https://www.cbeinternational.org/resource/article/priscilla-papers-academic-journal/uncovering-and-dismantling-barriers-women.

McClellan, Hannah. "Assemblies of God Ordains Record Number of Women." News & Reporting (Christianity Today, August 5, 2022). Accessed August 10, 2022. https://www.christianitytoday.com/news/2022/august/assemblies-god-ordain-women-record.html.

McKnight, Scot. *The Blue Parakeet: Rethinking How You Read the Bible.* 2nd ed. Grand Rapids, MI: Zondervan, 2018.

McPherson, Aimee Semple. "Fishers of Men." In *The Collected Sermons and Writings of Aimee Semple McPherson* Vol. 2. North Charleston, SC: CreateSpace Independent Publishing, 2015.

———. "International Church of the Foursquare Gospel." Declaration of Faith. Accessed August 1, 2022. https://foursquare-leader.s3.us-east-1.amazonaws.com/about_us/business/Bylaws_English_2019.pdf.

———. "Foursquare Gospel World-Wide Missions," *The Bridal Call Foursquare* 11 (October 1927): 15.

———. "The Servants and the Handmaidens." *The Bridal Call Foursquare* 13, no. 9 (February 1930): 5-6.

———. *Real Aimee.* Los Angeles: Foursquare Media, 2022.

Mead, Patrick. "Who 'Killed' Junia? Part One." The Junia Project. April 30, 2014. Accessed July 15, 2022. https://juniaproject.com/who-killed-junia-part-one/.

———. "Who 'Killed' Junia? Part Two." The Junia Project. May 2, 2014. Accessed July 15, 2022. https://juniaproject.com/who-killed-junia-part-two/.

Messner, Matt. "Reasons Women Should Lead." Priscilla Papers. CBE International. Accessed April 30, 2000. https://www.cbeinternational.org/resource/article/priscilla-papers-academic-journal/reasons-women-should-lead.

Midgley, Claire, Gabriela DeBues-Stafford, Penelope Lockwood, and Sabrina Thai. "She Needs to See It to Be It: The Importance of Same-Gender Athletic Role Models." *Sex Roles* 85, no. 3 (August 2021). ResearchGate. Accessed August 31, 2022. https://www.researchgate.net/publication/348256035_She_Needs_to_See_it_to_be_it_The_Importance_of_Same-Gender_Athletic_Role_Models.

Mishra, Nita. "What Do We Mean When We Speak about Equality, Diversity, and Inclusion in a University Institution?" UCC. May 19, 2022. Accessed August 31, 2022. https://www.ucc.ie/en/research/about/.

Morris, Henry M. *The Genesis Record: A Scientific and Devotional Commentary on The Book of Beginnings.* Grand Rapids, MI: Baker Book House, 2009.

Moulton, W. F., and A. S. Geden. *A Concordance to the Greek Testament.* Edinburgh: T & T. Clark, 1897).

Mounce, William D. *Mounce's Complete Expository Dictionary of Old & New Testament Words.* Grand Rapids, MI: Zondervan, 2006.

National Center for Education Statistics. "Fast Facts: Degrees Conferred by Race/Ethnicity and Sex (2018-19)." Accessed August 31, 2022. https://nces.ed.gov/fastfacts/display.asp?id=72.

Neufeld, Kathleen Rempel. "Caught by the Fence: Challenges Facing Women in Ministry Leadership in the Mennonite Brethren Church." Order No. NR79979, Edmonton, Alberta, St. Stephen's College (Canada), 2010. In PROQUESTMS Religion Database, https://www.proquest.com/dissertations-theses/caught-fence-challenges-facing-women-ministry/docview/889078901/se-2?accountid=40702.

Ng, Sarabeth. "Christ's Permission above All Else." CBE International. June 5, 2022. Accessed May 9, 2022. https://www.cbeinternational.org/resource/article/mutuality-blog-magazine/christs-permission-above-all-else.

Niemala, Kati. "Female Clergy as Agents of Religious Change?" *Religions* 2, no. 3 (2011): 358-71. https://doi.org/10.3390/rel2030358

Nixdorff, Janet L., and Theodore H. Rosen. "The Glass Ceiling Women Face: An Examination and Proposals for Development of Future Women Entrepreneurs." *New England Journal of Entrepreneurship* 13, no. 2 (Fall 2010): 71-87. https://www.proquest.com/scholarly-journals/glass-ceiling-women-face-examination-proposals/docview/862750175/se-2?accountid=40702.

Oakes, Anna. "Amid Growth in Leadership, One-Fifth of U.S. Clergy Are Female." Watauga Democrat. March 1, 2020. Accessed August 3, 2022. https://www.wataugademocrat.com/community/amid-growth-in-leadership-one-fifth-of-u-s-clergy-are-female/article_739b14a1-212a-5d06-b429-4d888a369255.html.

Olson, Laura R., Sue E. S. Crawford, and James L. Guth. "Changing Issue Agendas of Women Clergy." *Society for Scientific Study of Religion* 39, no. 2 (June 2000): 140-53. https://www.jstor.org/stable/1387499.

Palmer, Phoebe. *Promise of the Father; or, A Neglected Specialty of the Last Days: Addressed to the Clergy and Laity of All Christian communities.* 1859. Repr. Salem: Schmul Publishers, 1981.

"Pastor Demographics and Statistics: Number of Pastors in the US." Zippia (The Career Expert). Accessed August 10, 2022. https://www.zippia.com/pastor-jobs/demographics.

"Patriarchy." Merriam-Webster Dictionary. Accessed January 2, 2023. https://www.merriam-webster.com/dictionary/patriarchy.

Pavalko, Eliza K., Krysia N. Mossakowski, and Vanessa J. Hamilton. "Does Perceived Discrimination Affect Health? Longitudinal Relationships between Work Discrimination and Women's Physical and Emotional Health." *Journal of Health and Social Behavior* 44, no. 1 (March 2003): 18-33. https://www.proquest.com/scholarly-journals/does-perceived-discrimination-affect-health/docview/201660688/se-2?accountid=40702.

Payne, Leah. *Gender and Pentecostal Revivalism: Making a Female Ministry in the Early Twentieth Century.* New York: Palgrave MacMillan, 2015.

———. "Why Foursquare's Female Leaders Have It Harder Today." ChristianityToday.com. CT Women, May 29, 2019. Accessed August 3, 2022. https://www.christianitytoday.com/ct/2019/may-web-only/foursquare-church-aimee-semple-mcpherson-tammy-dunahoo.html.

Payne, Philip Barton, and Vince Huffaker. *Why Can't Women Do That?: Breaking down the Reasons Churches Put Men in Charge.* Boulder, CO: Vinati Press, 2021.

Payne, Sean, and Susan Barnett. "PC(USA) Minister Survey: Discrimination, Opportunity, and Struggles of Leadership Report." Presbyterian Mission Agency. 2021. Accessed August 10, 2022. https://www.presbyterianmission.org/wp-content/uploads/Minister-Descrimination-Opportunity-and-Struggles-of-Leadership-Report-copy.pdf.

Pederson, Rena. "Paul Praises a Woman Apostle." CBE International. Accessed June 11, 2022. https://www.cbeinternational.org/resource/article/paul-praises-woman-apostle.

The People of the United Methodist Church. "Book of Resolutions: Every Barrier Down: toward Full Embrace of All Women in Church and Society." The United Methodist Church. Accessed August 27, 2022. http://www.umc.org/en/content/book-of-resolutions-every-barrier-down-toward-full-embrace-of-all-women-in-church-and-society. (From *The Book of Resolutions of The United Methodist Church*. Copyright © 2016 by The United Methodist Publishing House. Used by permission.)

Pierce, Ronald W., Rebecca Merrill Groothuis, and Gordon D. Fee. *Discovering Biblical Equality: Complementarity without Hierarchy*. Leicester: InterVarsity Press, 2005.

Percupchick, Harry. "Women in Leadership: Understanding Potential Drivers/Restrainers of Female Progression in the Workplace." Order No. 3467494. Doctor of Management in Organizational Leadership diss., University of Phoenix, 2011. https://www.proquest.com/openview/6fd83489f0fc7dde5f7b71798288287d/1?pq-origsite=gscholar&cbl=18750.

Piper, John. "Is There a Place for Female Professors at Seminary?" January 22, 2018 (audio and transcript). Desiring God. Accessed August 3, 2022, https://www.desiringgod.org/interviews/is-there-a-place-for-female-professors-at-seminary.

Porterfield, Jennifer and Brian H. Kleiner. "A New Era: Women and Leadership." *Equal Opportunities International* 24, no. 5 (2005): 49-56. https://www.proquest.com/scholarly-journals/new-era-women-leadership/docview/199569439/se-2?accountid=40702.

Preato, Dennis J. "Junia, a Female Apostle: An Examination of the Historical Record." CBE International. April 25, 2019. Accessed June 2, 2020. https://www.cbeinternational.org/resource/article/priscilla-papers-academic-journal/junia-female-apostle-examination-historical.

The Presbyterian Outlook. "The Rise of Women in the Pulpit." The Presbyterian Outlook. Accessed October 8, 2022, https://pres-outlook.org/2019/10/the-rise-of-women-in-the-pulpit.

Prime, Jeanine, and Corinne A. Moss-Racusin. "Engaging Men in Gender Initiatives: What Change Agents Need to Know (Report)." Catalyst, May 4, 2009. Accessed August 31, 2022. https://www.catalyst.org/research/engaging-men-in-gender-initiatives-what-change-agents-need-to-know/.

"Prominent Biblical Scholars on Women in Ministry." Marg Mowczko. January 25, 2022. June 2, 2022. https://margmowczko.com/prominent-biblical-scholars-on-women-in-ministry.

"Resources." The Foursquare Church. Accessed April 05, 2021. https://www.foursquare.org/resources.

Qualls, Joy E. A. *God Forgive Us for Being Women: Rhetoric, Theology, and the Pentecostal Truth*. Eugene, OR: Pickwick Publications, 2018.

Redford, Douglas. *The Pentateuch*. Vol. 1 of *Standard Reference Library: Old Testament*. Cincinnati, OH: Standard Publishing, 2008.

Reyburn, William David, and Euan McG. Fry. "A Handbook on Genesis." Swindon, England: United Bible Societies Handbook Series, 1997.

Reynolds, Leighton Durham, and Nigel Guy Wilson. *Scribes and Scholars: A Guide to the Transmission of Greek and Latin Literature*. 3rd ed. Oxford: Clarendon Press, 1991.

Richards, Lawrence O. *The Teacher's Commentary*. Wheaton, IL: Victor Books, 1982.

Riley, Claudette. "Assemblies of God Selects First Woman Executive in 100+ Years." News-Leader. April 30, 2018. Accessed August 3, 2022.

https://www.news-
leader.com/story/news/local/ozarks/now/2018/04/30/assemblies-god-
selects-first-woman-executiveassemblies-god-hires-female-executive-first-
time-100-yea/564494002/.

Robert, Dana L. "World Christianity as a Women's Movement." *International Bulletin of Missionary Research* 30, issue 4 (October 2006), 180-86, 188. https://www.proquest.com/scholar-journals/world-christianity-as-womens-movement/docview/216012504/se-2?accountid=4072. https://doi.org/10.1177/239693930603000403

Rockwell, Sam, ed. *Identity Keystones: What Makes Us Foursquare.* Los Angeles, CA: The Foursquare Church, 2017.

Romey, Linda. "It's Time to Find out Where Religious Life Can Go without Patriarchy." Global Sisters Report. January 18, 2022. Accessed August 31, 2022. https://www.globalsistersreport.org/news/religious-life/column/its-time-find-out-where-religious-life-can-go-without-patriarchy.

Rose, Floyd E. *An Idea Whose Time Has Come.* Columbus, GA: Brentwood Christian Press, 2002.

Schell, Steve. ed. *Women in Leadership Ministry.* Los Angeles: Foursquare Media, 2007.

Schleifer, Cyrus, and Amy D. Miller. "Occupational Gender Inequality among American Clergy, 1997-2016: Revisiting the Stained-Glass Ceiling." *Sociology of Religion* 78, no 4 (Winter, 2017): 387-410, https://www.proquest.com/scholarly-journals/occupational-gender-inequality-among-american/docview/2266356251/se-2?accountifd=40702.

Schmithals, Walter. *The Office of Apostle in the Early Church.* Translated by John E Steely. New York: Abingdon, 1969.

Scholer, David M. *Male Headship: God's Intention or Man's Invention.* Berkeley, CA: WATCHword, 1988.

———. *Women in Early Christianity.* 14th ed. New York: Garland Pub., 1983.

Scott, Halee G. "Perceptions of Christian Women Leaders in Church-Related Organizations." *Christian Educational Journal* 11, no. 1 (May 2014): 52-70. https://doi.org/10.1177/073989131401100105

Segal, Eliezer. "A Dubious Blessing." University of Calvary. Accessed August 3, 2022. http://people.ucalgary.ca/~elsegal/Shokel/991021_DubiousBlessing.html.

Shehan, Constance L., Marsha Wiggins, and Susan Coy-Rydzewski. "Responding to and Retreating from the Call: Career Salience, Work Satisfaction, and Depression among Clergywomen." *Pastoral Psychology* 55, no 5 (May 2007): 637-43. https://www.proquest.com/scholarly-journals/responding-rereating-call-career-salience-work/docview/756818379/se-2?accountid=40702.

Shellnutt, Kate. "Justice Department Investigates Southern Baptist Convention over Abuse." News & Reporting. Christianity Today. August 12, 2022. Accessed August 31, 2022. https://www.christianitytoday.com/ncws/2022/august/federal-investigation-southern-baptist-abuse-executive-comm.html.

Siddur Ashkenaz. "Weekday. *Shacharit.* Preparatory Prayers. Morning Blessings 2-4." *Sefaria.* Accessed January 3, 2023. https://www.sefaria.org/sheets/119367?lang=bi.

Silliman, Daniel. "Foursquare Abuse Response Ignites Fight over Transparency." News & Reporting. Christianity Today, August 4, 2022. Accessed August 31, 2022. https://www.christianitytoday.com/news/2022/august/foursquare-abuse-transparency-ignite-grace-larkin-lpu.html.

Simon, Rita J., and Pamela S. Nadell. "In the Same Voice or Is It Different? Gender and the Clergy." *Sociology of Religion* 56, no. 1 (Spring, 1995): 63. https://www.proquest.com/scholarly-journals/same-voice-is-different-gender-clergy/docview/216771333/se-2?accountid=40702.

Smith, Mindy. "Her Story: Forming a Woman's Voice in the Pulpit." D.Min. diss. Newberg, OR: George Fox University, 2018. http://digitalcommons.georgefox.edu/dmin/246.

Stark, Rodney. "Reconstructing the Rise of Christianity: The Role of Women." *Sociology of Religion* 56, no. 3 (Fall, 1995): 229. https://www.proquest.com/scholarly-journals/reconstructing-rise-christianity-role-women/docview/216768018/se-2?accountid=40702.

Stein, Robert H. *The New American Commentary Series.* 42 Vols. Logos Bible Software. 1992. https://www.logos.com/product/55024/the-new-american-commentary-series.

Stephenson, Lisa P. *Dismantling the Dualisms for American Pentecostal Women in Ministry: A Feminist-Pneumatological Approach.* Vol. 9 of Global Pentecostal and Charismatic Studies. Leiden: Brill, 2012.

———. "Prophesying Women and Ruling Men: Women's Religious Authority in North American Pentecostalism." *Religions* 2, no. 3 (2011): 410-26, https://www.proquest.com/scholarly-journals/prophesying-women-ruling-men-womens-religious/docview/1537382956/se-2?accountid=40702.

Stevens, Lesley. "Different Voice/Different Voices: Anglican Women in Ministry." *Review of Religious Research* 30, no. 3 (March 1989): 262-75. JSTOR. Accessed August 3, 2022. https://www.jstor.org/stable/3511511.

Stott, John. *Issues Facing Christians Today.* 4th ed. Grand Rapids, MI: Zondervan, 2006.

Sutton, Matthew Avery. *Aimee Semple McPherson and the Resurrection of Christian America.* Cambridge, MA: Harvard University Press, 2009.

Swidler, Leonard J. *Biblical Affirmations of Women.* Philadelphia: The Westminster Press, 1979.

———. "Jesus Was a Feminist." God's Word to Women. January 1971. Accessed July 15, 2022. https://www.godswordtowomen.org/feminist.htm.

Tal, Diana, and Avishag Gordon. "Women as Political Leaders: A Bibliometric Analysis of the Literature." *Society* 55, no. 3 (June 2018): 256-61, https://www.proquest.com/scholarly-journals/women-as-political-leaders-bibliometric-analysis/docview/2036586925/se-2?accountid=40702.

The Foursquare Church. "2017 Cabinet Report." Accessed July 3, 2022. http://s3.amazonaws.com/foursquare-org/assets/Cabinet_2017_NCO_Report.pdf.

The People of the United Methodist Church. "Book of Resolutions: Every Barrier Down: Toward Full Embrace of All Women in Church and Society." The United Methodist Church. Accessed August 27, 2019. http://www.umc.org/en/content/book-of-resolutions-every-barrier-down-toward-full-embrace-of-all-women-in-church-and-society.

The Presbyterian Outlook. "The Rise of Women in the Pulpit." The Presbyterian Outlook. Accessed October 8, 2019. https://pres-outlook.org/2019/10/the-rise-of-women-in-the-pulpit.

"The Qualities That Distinguish Women Leaders." Caliper. 2005. Accessed August 31, 2022. http://www.calipermedia.calipercorp.com/whitepapers/us/Qualities-in-Women-Leaders.pdf.

"This is Foursquare: Cabinet Report 2022." Foursquare Leader. Accessed August 3, 2022. https://foursquare-leader.s3.us-east-1.amazonaws.com/about_us/business/2022-Cabinet-Report.pdf.

Thomas, Lyola. "A Template for the Future: Resonant Leadership in the Song of Deborah." *Journal of International Women's Studies* 22, no. 6 (June 2021): 3-10, https://www.proquest.com/scholarly-journals/template-future-resonant-leadership-song-deborah/docview/2550694638/se-2.

Thompson, Rowan M. "Advancing Equity, Diversity, and Inclusion: A How-to Guide." Physics Today. March 10, 2022. Accessed August 31, 2022. https://doi.org/10.1063/PT.3.4921.

Thorley, John. *Junia, a Woman Apostle*. Leiden: E. J. Brill, 1996.

Times Higher Education. "World University Rankings." Times Higher Education (THE). Accessed June 8, 2022. https://www.timeshighereducation.com/world-university-rankings/2022/world-ranking#!/page/0/length/25/sort_by/rank/sort_order/asc/cols/stats.

Tremper, Karen. "Advancing Women in Senior Leadership." In *Identity Keystones: What Makes Us Foursquare*, edited by Sam Rockwell, 58-81. Los Angeles, CA: The Foursquare Church, 2017.

―――. "Credentialed Women in the Foursquare Church: An Exploration of Opportunities and Hindrances in Leadership" PhD diss., Fuller Theological Seminary, 2013.

Truman, Althea. "The Lived Experience of Leadership for Female Pastors in Religious Organizations." PhD diss., Capella University, 2010. https://search.proquest.com/docview/753892386.

Tyagi, S. "The Benefit of More Women in Leadership Roles." Women of HR. April 28, 2016. Accessed August 31, 2022. http://womenofhr.com/the-benefit-of-more-women-in-leadership-roles.

Tyra, Gary. *The Holy Spirit in Mission: Prophetic Speech and Action in Christian Witness*. Downers Grove, IL: IVP Academic, 2011.

Van Cleave, Nathaniel. *The Vine and the Branches: A History of the International Church of the Foursquare Gospel*. Los Angeles: International Church of the Foursquare Gospel, 1992.

Vanauken, Phil. "Understanding Church Burnout." June 2022. Accessed August 31, 2022. https://business.baylor.edu/Phil_vanauken/ChurchBurnout.html.

"Video: 'Women in Leadership Ministry' Series with Jerry Dirmann." News + Resources, January 30, 2020. Accessed August 31, 2022. https://resources.foursquare.org/video/video-women-in-leadership-ministry-series-with-jerry-dirmann/.

Whitehead, Deborah. "Women Lead Religious Groups in Many Ways—Besides the Growing Number Who Have Been Ordained." Colorado Arts and Sciences Magazine, January 19, 2022. Accessed August 31, 2022.

https://www.colorado.edu/asmagazine/2022/01/19/women-lead-religious-groups-many-ways-besides-growing-number-who-have-been-ordained.

Williams, Terran. *How God Sees Women: The End of Patriarchy*. Cape Town South Africa: The Spiritual Bakery Publications, 2022.

———. "Resolving Five Complementarian Protests to Priscilla the Pastor-Teacher." CBE International. June 5, 2022. Accessed July 6, 2022. https://www.cbeinternational.org/resource/article/mutuality-blog-magazine/resolving-five-complementarian-protests-priscilla-pastor.

"Willow Creek Promises Investigation amid New Allegations Against Bill Hybels." Christianity Today. April 21, 2019. Accessed January 4, 2023. https://www.christianitytoday.com/news/2018/april/bill-hybels-willow-creek-promises-investigation-allegations.html.

Wirth, Linda. *Breaking through the Glass Ceiling: Women in Management*. Geneva, Switzerland: International Labour Office, 2001.

Witherington, Ben. "Why Arguments Against Women in Ministry Aren't Biblical." Patheos. June 2, 2015. Accessed July 12, 2022. https://www.patheos.com/blogs/bibleandculture/2015/06/02/why-arguments-against-women-in-ministry-arent-biblical/.

———. *Women and the Genesis of Christianity*. Cambridge: Cambridge University Press, 1999.

"Women Are Doing Their Part. Now Companies Need to Do Their Part, Too." Women in the Workplace Study 2018. Accessed August 31, 2022. https://womenintheworkplace.com/2018#!.

"Women in Ministry Leadership Resources." News + Resources, February 5, 2022. https://resources.foursquare.org/link/women-in-ministry-leadership-resources/.

"Women in Scripture and Mission: Huldah." CBE International. Accessed May 20, 2022. https://www.cbeinternational.org/resource/audio/women-scripture-and-mission-hulda.

"Women in the Workplace 2021." LeanIn.Org and McKinsey & Company. Accessed July 12, 2022. https://womenintheworkplace.com/.

Wright, N. T. "Women's Service in the Church: The Biblical Basis." Conference Paper, St John's College, Durham, September 4, 2004.

York, Jessica. "Antoinette Brown and Olympia Brown." Signs of Our Faith Series. 2013. Unitarian Universalist Association. July 21, 2017. Accessed August 10, 2022. https://www.uua.org/re/tapestry/children/signs/session16/288929.shtml.

Ziegenhals, Gretchen E. "Women in Ministry: Beyond the Impasse." Baylor University Center for Christian Ethics. 2009. Accessed July 13, 2022. https://www.baylor.edu/content/services/document.php/98766.pdf.

Zikmund, Barbara B., Adair T. Lummis, and Patricia M. Yin Chang. *Clergy Women: An Uphill Calling*. Westminster John Knox Press. Louisville, KY: 1998.

Ziv, Stav. "7 Striking Facts about Women in the Workplace." The Muse. June 19, 2020. Accessed August 31, 2022. https://www.themuse.com/advice/7-striking-facts-women-in-the-workplace-2018.

Made in the USA
Middletown, DE
07 June 2023

32243891R00124